The Whole Duty of Man

IN TODAY'S ENGLISH BY

Michael Perry

ARK PUBLISHING
130 City Road, London EC1V 2NJ

All special material in, and the text of, this abridgement,
© Ark Publishing 1980.
First published by Ark Publishing,
130 City Road, London EC1V 2NJ.

ISBN 0 86201 104 3

ISBN 0 86201 107 8   Cased edition

Typesetting: Nuprint Services Ltd, Harpenden, Herts.
Printed in England by McCorquodale (Newton) Ltd.,
        Newton-le-Willows, Lancashire.

CONTENTS

SECTION TWO: *Our duty to ourselves*

PUBLISHER'S PREFACE

In making available to a new readership *The Whole Duty of Man* in Michael Perry's dynamically revised version, we are republishing one of the most remarkable books of English Christianity. It stands with the *Book of Common Prayer, The Pilgrim's Progress* and other classics. For more than a century it was a necessary part of any literate Christian's bookshelf in the English church; and when non-conformity introduced other churches than the Anglican church into English society, the book remained popular and useful in the face of many imitators and competitors.

Quite simply, it is a compendium of the Christian life. 'Duty', for its author, meant the natural behaviour of a Christian in all areas of existence. If your soul is right, he argues, then you will demonstrate that by your actions in the most everyday things. So the author deals with temperance, loyalty, fair trading, modesty, parents, employer-employee relations, and many other topics.

The England of its author was in some ways not very different to England today. Its social problems frequently mirror our own, as for example with the appalling extent of alcohol abuse (which John Wesley was to comment upon not long afterwards), and its counterpart in present-day problems especially in the young. The author's comments on this, as on poverty, work, and a host of other familiar problem-areas, are as biblically-based and therefore as relevant as the time they were written.

He was an Anglican, a member of the only legal church in England of his day: in this edition, some specifically Anglican passages have been abridged in order to widen the scope of the book. It has not been possible (and we would not wish) to disguise the denominational origin of the book, and the author's comments on church structures and ordinances are made against his particular background. In addition, the author was not primarily a theologian, and does not set out to give a systematic theology of all the matters he raises. Thus his remarks on the Old Testament covenant, for example, should be read in the light of the point he is making, rather than as a fully worked-out treatment.

The central point of the book *is* stated comprehensively and forcefully, and makes the book as relevant today as ever. The whole duty of man, says the author, is to fear and obey God. But the miraculous truth of the matter is that God has made this impossible task possible – and pleasurable – by giving us his Son and the grace of the Holy Spirit. Love of God's Son, the book urges, is man's whole duty and joy.

*   *   *

The text of this edition has been modernised to reinstate the clarity and directness of the original. To be consistent with the tone of the text, Michael Perry has replaced the author's quotations from the Authorised Version of the Bible by the most appropriate modern version of the text in each case, modified in some cases by reference to the original. The debt owed to current versions is gladly acknowledged.

EDITOR'S PREFACE

'The Whole Duty of Man' soon became everyone's home tutor for the Christian Faith. It dealt plainly and simply with moral duties and had very wide influence on people's attitudes and behaviour – far more so than any one religious book might have today. As with other literary and artistic successes, there were many imitators. But nothing quite achieved the stature or the success of the 'Whole Duty'. There was no author's name on the document when it appeared in 1657, but a preface 'Letter to the Bookseller' signed by John Hammond, an Oxford Fellow. It's just possible that he could have been the author of the book, but the name of Allestree, Doctor and Regius Professor of Divinity at Oxford is favoured.

As the book itself makes clear, it was designed for the 'average reader'. Today it would take a considerable theological background and a fair knowledge of English to interpret it accurately. So there is every reason to update its language and make it readable again.

As to the faults of the 'The Whole Duty', they were early acknowledged. It was criticised for over-emphasis on the 'doing' of religion, too little on the power of God's forgiveness in Christ. Nevertheless, many like Wesley and Simeon, for whom grace was central to the faith, held the 'Whole Duty' in high regard and were dramatically influenced by it. Perhaps a book on Christian behaviour will inevitably concentrate overmuch on 'works', rewards, and punishments for failure. What saves 'The Whole Duty' is the essential place given to the expression of God's love in Jesus' sacrifice at Calvary, and the dependence of all our hopes on that one act of redemption (see 'Introduction', 'At his Table', 'Love and Forgiveness', etc.)

The great value of the 'The Whole Duty' for today is it's deep – sometimes psychological – insights into the attitudes which govern our behaviour. It knows us too well to let us get away with anything, it reveals God's sovereignty, appeals to wisdom, sense and logic, and shows us the path to serenity and Christian maturity. Especially noteworthy is the author's thorough knowledge and pertinent use of the Bible. The book becomes an exposition of relevant Bible passages, so that not only the average reader, but also the Bible student and teacher have a resource book in their hands.

MICHAEL PERRY

Introduction

LOOK AFTER YOUR SOULS!

The single purpose of this book is to be a straight forward and short lesson for the average reader; teaching him how he might live now and be happy in eternity. But there is no point in telling people what they ought to do unless they are convinced of the reasons. So, before I start listing the details of proper Christian behaviour, I have to try to establish the underlying logic – that of taking care of your own soul.

You can look at a person in two ways: physically and spiritually – the body and the soul. The body is only the visible aspect of the whole – just so much flesh, liable to pain and decay. After death, the body is not tolerated above the ground but buried in order to rot; so much for its value. Yet, what care we take of the lesser part of us! While the more precious part – the soul – nobody bothers about, and it becomes neglected.

Here lies the root of all the sins we commit: our carelessness about our souls. So whoever wants to walk the Christian way, must put this right first. It doesn't need scholarship, or special skills. The ordinary man – so long as he is not a complete fool – has enough wisdom to care for his soul. He needs only the same reasoning that he applies to his practical life.

What I am going to do is to list four things which motivate us to take care in our everyday lives, and suggest the effect the same considerations ought to have upon our care of the soul.

First of all, *value*. If something is valuable, we watch it carefully and make sure that we do not lose it. Nobody puts *rubbish* in the bank! It is the precious things we care about. And doesn't the soul deserve more care than everything else put together? It's worth infinitely more: first, because it's made in the image of God.

The Lord God took some soil from the ground and formed a man out of it; he breathed life-giving breath into his nostrils and the

11

man became a living being. (Genesis 2.7)

In the second place, *lasting worth*. It's the lasting things which we count more important. Now the soul is a thing which will last for ever; when wealth, beauty, strength – our bodies themselves, fade away. The soul never dies. So, in this respect too, the soul is of great worth. Aren't we mad to neglect it! We can spend days, weeks, months, years – our whole lives – hunting after a fraction of the wealth of this world which is of no lasting value, and all the time be letting the one enduring treasure – our soul – be stolen from us by the devil.

Then, the more useful something is, the more we miss it. So *common sense* teaches us to take great care. We don't panic if a hair falls out. The threat of losing an eye or a limb is a very different matter; we take much more care because we know how miserable we would be without them. But in all the world there is no worse misery than losing one's soul. What good is it to pamper our bodies and consign our souls to flames in eternity?

Danger compels us very quickly to take care. The soul is in a great deal of danger. The very first thing we do for our souls is to vow a continual war against the world, the flesh and the devil. And whoever makes any truce with these three is a traitor to his soul, and a promise-breaker. Don't forget it! Let's have a look at the calibre of these enemies.

A wartime enemy is to be feared for subtlety and cunning. The Genesis chapter 3 story of the fruit tree in the garden is sufficient illustration of how cunning our enemy is. In a physical war we might well fear the enemy's alertness and vigilence; in the spiritual war these are the devil's stock-in-trade!

You be alert, be on the watch! Your enemy, the devil, roams round like a roaring lion, looking for someone to devour. (1 Peter 5.8)

He watches every opportunity to gain the advantage against us. And he is so careful, he certainly won't let one chance slip by him.

Then again, the enemy close by is much more of a threat than the one far away. The distance which divides us and our enemies gives us time to arm and to prepare ourselves. But the enemy on our borders can catch us unawares. And the flesh is this sort of enemy – the 'enemy at the gates'; no, worse than that, it's a fifth column already amongst us and close to the seat of power! Another thing to be afraid of is a false show of friendship. Beneath it lurks malice. And it hurts! The flesh offers us a desirable bait of pleasures and delights, and catches us on the barbed hook. If we bite, we are lost!

Then what about the numerical strength of our enemy? The world is a vast army ranged against us. There is nothing of what the world offers, no state in which we find ourselves, which does not at some time make war on our souls: honours can bring pride, wealth can bring greed, prosperity makes us forget God, and set-backs make us blame him. Food can make us gluttons, drink can make us drunken fools. Even the company we keep can entice us to sin.

When you think about it, isn't having a drowsy soul quite a risk? It's no good saying, 'We'll wake up when we've got to.' That's how Delilah woke Samson when the Philistines were right on top of him – too late!

> If the owner of a house knew the time when the thief would come, you could be sure that he would stay awake and not let the thief break into his house. (Matthew 24.43)

And if you are surrounded by thieves, you have to keep a look out for them all the time. Are we wise enough to take that sort of care for our souls? How dangerous are our soul's enemies! And we can't even keep watch one hour – as Jesus said to his disciples (Matthew 26.40). And how determined are our soul's enemies! What hope is there if we forget God? How vulnerable we are!

But there is another way that our souls may be in danger – they may fall sick. As with the body and its organs, so with the soul: you can tell it's diseased when it doesn't function properly. How should we diagnose?

Divide the soul into understanding, will, and affections. Look for proof of disorder.

Not much knowledge of spiritual things? – understanding defective.

Tendency to want wrong rather than right? – mind twisted.

Strong desires for sin, and weak desires for God? – disorder of the affections.

How about the cure? Well, first find the cause of the sickness. How did the soul come into this diseased condition? I shall tell you, very briefly.

In Adam – Genesis 2 – we see man as God first created him, his soul filled with the knowledge of his duty and with the strength of character which would help him do it. And here is the agreement: if man obeys God, then his soul stays strong and there is no death, but eternal happiness. But breaking this 'covenant' means that mankind loses the full knowledge and the perfect strength which gives the power to do all that God requires. Then there is only death and fierce judgement to come.

What has happened to us all is shown in the story of Genesis 3. We have lost our knowledge and our strength. Our sick stomach rejects good food and our diseased soul craves for all the wrong things. So you see how we got this illness; and more – that it is likely to prove fatal. I presume I do not need to say anymore to convince you that our souls are in danger?

THE 'SECOND COVENANT'

But don't despair, there is hope of recovery for,

> Just as all people die because of their union with Adam, in the same way all will be raised to life because of their union with Christ. (1 Corinthians 15.22)

What does Christ do? First, he is our *prophet*. We find in the Gospels his instructions and his commandments. Our duty here is to listen to him, and to be ready and willing to learn all that God is revealing through him.

Second, he is our *priest*. Christ satisfied God for our sins. He obtains for us forgiveness and God's favour. He claims us back from hell's possession and sin's everlasting punishment. It was his death that achieved this; he offered himself up for the sins of those who repent with all their hearts, and change their ways. He is our priest because a priest offers sacrifices for the sins of the people. What part do we play? We make sure that we are sorry with all our heart. We break with sin – that has to come before forgiveness. We firmly believe in what Jesus has done. All our sins – however great – may be forgiven, and we'll be saved from the penalties due. Christ is our priest in another way too: he blesses and prays for us. He pleads for us at God's right hand (Romans 8.34). We must not resist his good will; we must allow ourselves to be turned from our sins.

Then, Christ strengthens us. First, he makes the law less rigid, requiring now that we honestly and genuinely try to do what good we can. And where we fail he accepts our sincere repentance. More, he sends his Holy Spirit into our lives to direct and instruct us, to give us power to overcome the tempting pull of sin. So he is our *king*. Kings govern and rule and put down their enemies. For our part we give ourselves – his obedient subjects – to be governed and ruled by him, to obey his wishes, to use his strength and power to subdue our sins, and not to rebel.

Finally, he has bought a glorious eternity for us – the kingdom of heaven. And he has gone to get it ready. We don't want to miss anthing of this, and we certainly will if we go on sinning without a care. So we have got to change our attitudes, to long for higher things:

> You have been raised to life with Christ, so set your hearts on the things that are in heaven where Christ sits on his throne at the right-hand side of God. Keep your minds fixed on things there, not on things here on earth. For you have died, and your life is hidden with Christ, and when he appears, then you will appear with him and share his glory. (Colossians 3.1-4)

So, you see, Christ is prophet, priest and king: prophet to teach, king to rule, priest to save. Then don't let us give up in despair; Christ can save our souls! If he hadn't redeemed them, they might not have been worth bothering about. But God has planned that by taking due care of our souls we shall receive the full blessing of what Christ has done.

Suppose a doctor takes on a patient with a critical disease, then by his skill brings him out of it. The patient is certain to recover if only he takes care of himself and obeys the doctor's orders. Will the man be so tired of living as to refuse to co-operate? God gave his only Son – who left his glory and suffered death on the cross to keep our souls from dying. His Holy Spirit stays at our side looking after us with offers of his grace; grieved when we do not accept (Ephesians 4.30). Could we treat God in a more spiteful way than to refuse this cure? These souls of ours – Christ thought them worthy of every drop of his blood. Shouldn't we look after them? And doesn't God who made our souls best know their value? Of course he does! And he prizes them highly. Do we respect his opinion? Then aren't we obliged to keep them from neglect? – especially now that nothing but our own carelessness can possibly destroy them?

Look after yourselves – look after your souls!

OBEY!

The blessing Jesus bought for us will make our souls happy – eternal happiness is just one of those blessings. But true happiness comes with obedience. We must honestly try to obey the whole will of God. Then we need to know what the will of God is! There are those things that are so indelibly marked on our souls that we know them naturally – just like people who have never heard of the Bible but hold to the same general principles – being good, having respect for parents etc. As St Paul says in Romans 2.15, they have their consciences too.

Although Christ has brought greater light into the world, he never meant it to put out the natural light which God implanted in our souls. So don't do things which your natural conscience condemns. It's really very sad when Christians who let everybody know how religious they are, do things that non-Christians would never do. Here's a foundation principle: no religious practice or opinion comes from God if it permits wickedness.

Yet God reveals more of his will through the scriptures. Some commandments were given before Christ, for instance the 'Ten Commandments' (Deuteronomy 5; Exodus 20). Other commandments were given by Christ. He added much both to the law implanted in us by nature, and to that of the Old Testament. These commands of Christ we find in the New Testament – for instance, the 'Sermon on the Mount' in Matthew chapters 5, 6, and 7.

1

Our Duty to God

We must be
'sober, sensible, and self controlled.'
(Titus 2.2)

Let's start with our duty to God – that being the best foundation. To acknowledge God, is to believe in him as an infinite glorious Spirit, as he has always been – without beginning and without ending. He made us. He took responsibility for us and he bought us back from our sin. He can make us fit for his service. He is Father, Son and Holy Spirt – one God to be worshipped for ever. Nothing changes him. He is spiritual and invisible. No man has seen him or ever can see him (1 Timothy 6.16). He is great and marvellous beyond anything we can imagine. Nothing made him, but he makes all things.

So much for what he is – now what he is like: he is infinitely good, kind, loving and truthful. He is infinitely just, wise and powerful. He rules over all things. He knows all things, and he is present everywhere.

But acknowledging him is not enough. He is God, and we have duties towards him: the first, is faith.

FAITH

Faith is believing not only in what he is, but also in what he says. He is truth, and what he says is true. We learn what he says by the Bible. In the Bible, we have the *witness* to his action (set out in stories), and also *doctrines* (that Christ is the Son of God, and so on). So the Scripture lays the foundation of Christian knowledge on which we may build a Christian life.

The Bible has *commandments* too. We are to believe that they come from God, and to obey them. The Bible has *warnings*. We must believe that they come from God and will apply to us if we are not sorry for the wrongs we do.

Then, the Bible contains *promises*. Such promises apply both to our bodies and our souls. God will provide for all our needs if we put him first.

> Be concerned above everything else with the Kingdom of God, and with what he requires of you, and he will provide you with these other things. (Matthew 6.33)

There are promises for the soul too:

> Take my yoke and put it on you, and learn from me, for I am gentle and humble in spirit; and then your souls will find rest. (Matthew 11.29)

The yoke was the beam across the back by which strong animals dragged along their loads. Jesus says that we ought to change our loads for his and we would find peace at heart. But note the condition: we must take on his yoke – become his servants and followers. It is the same with the other promises to the soul; always the conditions. There is pardon for those who repent, gifts of skill and character for those who make use of what they have been given already and humbly pray for more, completeness of spirit in eternity for those who go on obeying until the end.

If we believe God's promises, we will want to fulfil the conditions. Without fulfilling the conditions, we really can't expect to benefit by his promises. Would you deserve pay without work? More than this: one of the reasons for God giving us these promises is to encourage us to live a holy life. Isn't this partly why Christ came? – and all God's promises are summed up in Christ. Yes, of course, he did come to deal with our sin. But he also came to plant holiness in the world.

> God...sent him first to you, to bless you by making every one of you turn away from his wicked ways. (Acts 3.26)

> He gave himself for us to rescue us from all wickedness and to make us a pure people who belong to him alone and are eager to do good. (Titus 2.14)

Christ is the foundation of all the promises of God:

> For it is he who is the 'Yes' to all God's promises. (2 Corinthians 1.20)

and in order to obtain God's promises we must fulfil the conditions:

All these promises are made to us. Let us purify ourselves from everything that makes body or soul unclean and, let us be completely holy by living in awe of God. (2 Corinthians 7.1)

HOPE

Then we must also hope; we must expect the good things he has promised. Hope encourages us to be pure:

Everyone who has this hope in Christ keeps himself pure, just as Christ is pure. (1 John 3.3)

Hope keeps us from despair. Logically, the man who despairs of forgiveness goes on sinning. That way ends in destruction. But hope sets before us God's promises and shows us how to triumph. With hope's encouragement we do not give ourselves up for lost, but set about changing course.

In Luke 16, the prodigal son runs away from his father and wastes his money, yet is accepted by his father when he eventually comes home. He is forgiven as though he had never gone wrong. Why does Jesus tell this story? Because he wants to show how gladly God will receive us, however wrong we have been. We only need to come back to him with real sorrow for what is past, and the will to obey him in the future.

The angels of God rejoice over one sinner who repents. (Luke 15.10)

Whom would you rather please? – God and his angels? Or Satan and his demons? God, of course! Besides which, we face happiness with God but torture with Satan.

LOVE

Then, we owe God love. Why do we love someone? Because he is good and kind. And God is both these things. He is the most kind. He is the most good. God's goodnesss is like the sea; our goodness, – small rivulets flowing onto the beach. God's goodness is shown supremely in Jesus Christ, and also in all the things we receive from him daily. Shall we not love him, who is altogether lovely?

Those whom we love we wish to please. Jesus says, 'If you love me, you will obey my commandments (John 14.15)'. It is impossible to say we love God if we don't obey him. Then we must obey him enthusiastically, for we should love him with all our hearts. Do we?

When we love someone, we want to be with him. We want to talk to him. It's the same with God; praying and thinking about him, listening to what he has to say to us, sharing in the bread and wine – these are the things which will bring us an intimacy with him. But so many of us are slow and unwilling. How will God ever claim us as thosewho love him if we have such a distaste for his company? – if fear keeps us away from him, or embarrassment, or any other worldly thing. You would not believe somone loved you if they kept their distance from you. So don't pretend you love God while you won't come near him!

TRUST

To fear God is to have such respect for him that we do not offend him. We don't go out of our way to provoke powerful men – and God is more powerful than any man. If we are sensible we will fear God above all.

We need to trust God when we are in spiritual and physical dangers. We must pray to him. We must rely on him alone. Whatever happens, we must not try to get ourselves out of difficulty by committing any sin. If we did we would bring upon ourselves a greater danger:

> What will you gain if you win the whole world and lose your own soul? (Matthew 16.26)

Nothing in this world is so important that we must sin for it.

Then we must remember that God does not ask us to do anything without giving us the strength to do it. If we do our part, he will do his.

But we have our physical needs too; we must rely upon him for these. Jesus taught us to pray for our 'daily bread', to live in continual dependence upon God our Father. That doesn't mean we should be lazy and expect to be fed by miracles! No, God gives us the necessities of life through our honest work. Paul says,

> Whoever refuses to work shouldn't be allowed to eat. (2 Thessalonians 3.10)

and we might well think that God would say the same.

If we cannot work through illness or age, we can cheerfully rest in God. Peter says,

Leave all your worries with him, because he cares for you.
(1 Peter 5.7)

Jesus assures us,

> Do not start worrying: 'Where will my food come from? or my
> drink? or my clothes?' Your Father in heaven knows that you
> need all these things.... So do not worry about tomorrow; it will
> have enough worries of its own. There is no need to add to the
> troubles each day brings. (Matthew 6.31,32,34)

Look at it this way: by trusting God you oblige him to provide for
you. If we feel bound not to let down those who depend on us and
trust us, how much more does God!

Last of all, remember the peace that comes from trust. Trusting
in God frees us from the nagging anxieties which disturb our
minds, keep us awake, and eat into our hearts.

> Don't worry about anything, but in all your prayers ask God for
> what you need, always asking him with a thankful heart. And
> God's peace, which is far beyond human understanding, will
> keep your hearts and minds safe with Christ Jesus. (Philippians
> 4.5-7)

HUMILITY

Humility is knowing ourselves to be poor and ordinary, and
knowing God to be very great, so that we submit to him happily
and without pretence. We submit to his will and to his wisdom.

We respond to his will with obedience and patience. Proud
people don't obey, because to obey someone you have to admit that
he is more important than you. God is infinitely greater than we
are in our need and poverty. But if we can't see that, we will never
obey him as he deserves. If you intend to obey God absolutely, then
you must gain a sense of his absolute greatness. Think of him as
majestic and glorious. Think of what puny little creatures we are.
He is powerful enough to do anything. But we

> cannot make a single hair white or black.
> (Matthew 5.36)

He is infinitely pure and holy, while we have stained ourselves with
sin. He is consistent and unchanging, while we fluctuate every
minute. He lives forever, but,

when he takes away our breath we die and go back to the dust from which we came. (Psalm 104.29)

Think about it! If you do, you'll realise what a difference there is between God and man, and you'll have to say, as Job did,

Now I have seen you with my own eyes, so I am ashamed of all I have said and repent in dust and ashes. (Job 42.5,6)

When you have found enough humility to obey, hang on to it! You need it still, for it will keep you from being conceited about your achievements. Conceit is a curse to the best of us, and it makes us utterly unacceptable to God. Conceit reduced the Pharisee to less than the tax collector, because he boasted of his own piety:

I thank you, God, that I am not greedy, dishonest, or an adulterer, like everybody else. I thank you that I am not like that tax collector over there. I fast two days a week, and I give you a tenth of all my income. (Luke 18.11,12)

Nothing we are or can do compares with God's perfection and purity.

Even our best actions are filthy through and through. (Isaiah 64.6)

So, if we boast of our achievements, it's like a tramp bragging about his clothes! Jesus tells us,

When you have done all that you have been told to do, say 'We are ordinary servants, we have only done our duty.' (Luke 17.10)

PATIENCE

Patience is the part of Christian submissiveness that yields to whatever God sends. If your souls are dominated by an admiration for God and all that he is, it won't be possible for you to grumble about what he does.

You wouldn't think much of a child if he flew into a temper every time he was put right by his mother or father. But don't we do the same thing when we grudge and sulk about what happens to us? It's lack of humility and quite wrong; for God can do what he likes with his creatures. Besides, it's foolish, because God brings us through such suffering for good reason. He's not like a human father, losing his temper with his children. God only corrects us for our own good.

> The Lord is merciful and will not reject us for ever. He may bring us sorrow, but his love for us is sure and strong. He takes no pleasure in causing us grief and pain. (Lamentations 3.33)

It's our sinfulness which gives him every right and reason to punish us. Tenderly he deals with us. If a father sees his child stubborn and rebellious, spoiling his own life, the kindest thing he can do is to correct him. Would it be kind *not* to correct him? When God sees us being sinful, he can either stop loving us, and let us destroy ourselves; or he can go on loving us, and punish us to put us right. There's no other way. So we must be patient under his correction.

Because God cares for us, he sends problems – messages as it were – to call us back to himself. How stupid we are to grumble at pains which are meant to be kind. It is like insulting the doctor for prescribing medicine! If the doctor then left us to die of our illness, every one would know whose fault it was!

When life is hard, we need to be submissive and thankful; but that's not all. Hard times must bear fruit. And this is how. When troubles come, we must check up on ourselves, note what we are thinking and doing, see if there is any sin which would invite God to discipline us. If we find ourselves guilty in any way, we must go to him and humbly confess our sins, not returning to them for the rest of our lives.

Sometimes there is no obvious cause for our troubles. We must still be patient. Surely no one can hurt us without God allowing it; he deals with us indirectly, as well as directly. Patience that claims to submit to God, but can't take trouble from men, is a sham. You'll find in Job, if you read his book, a true example of patience. He took the theft of his property as humbly as he accepted the discipline of God. When you suffer at the hands of other people, however unjust that suffering may seem to you, it still is justice in God's sight. So don't retaliate with anger and revenge like everybody else. Humbly look to God, honouring his judgement, asking for forgiveness for anything you have done wrong – anything for which he might be punishing you. You should bear his reproach with patience and thanks until he decides to take it away. Say with Job, Blessed be the name of the Lord! (Job 1.21)

But there are two sides to Christian obedience. We don't only submit to his will, but also to his wisdom. God is infinitely wise, so whatever he does must be the best that can be done. It's true of what he commands us, and it's true of what he lets happen in our lives. We have to trust him even if we cannot understand what he is doing. We have to obey him however illogical his commands may seem to our human wisdom. God doesn't make mistakes. So, if he chooses our way for us, it can't be wrong. We are to moderate our ambitions and rest in God's plans for us – even if they are the last thing we would have wanted for ourselves. Once you appreciate how infinitely wise God is and how very foolish we are by his standards, you have to agree that God's choices are best. A child needs his parents to choose for him to avoid dangerous mistakes. If a child did everything he wanted, he would be continually cutting and burning himself. We are just like children – always wanting those things which would harm us if we had them. We want wealth, honour, beauty, etc. If we had them they would only trap us and we should be drawn in to sin by them. God, who knows everything, sees this even if we do not. So he keeps from us those things which he knows will hurt us – and it's kind of him to do it! So, when we are disappointed, let's be patient – and more – let's happily accept what comes, knowing that it's the best that can happen to us. For it is chosen by the unerring wisdom of our heavenly Father.

HONOURING GOD

Our duty is to respect God's great power and authority. The duty is inward, and outward; we exalt him in our hearts, honouring him most highly, and the outworking of this is to respect him openly by the lives we live. Honour requires appropriate behaviour. If we really respect him we will not offend him – especially since he sees everything, and there is no way of deceiving him. If we reverence him we must not do sinful things.

There are special ways in which God is honoured by the things we do:

HONOURING GOD IN CHURCH

First at the place of public worship, the Church building. It is not holy in itself, but because of the purpose for which it is used. So we have to be very careful about what else we do there. Jesus taught us this by driving out the money-changers and the traders in the temple, saying,

It is written in the scriptures that God said, 'My temple will be called a house of prayer', but you are making it a hideout for thieves! (Matthew 21.12; John 2.16)

Churches are to be used only for the service of God and we are to go for that purpose only. The 'Preacher' of the Old Testament says, 'Watch your step when you go into the house of God!' (Ecclesiastes 5.1). In Church, then, your job is to talk with God. Shut out thoughts of the busy world – even the most innocuous thoughts. At any other time they are quite proper, but here they are sinful. If you go to worship with other motives, you are like Judas who pretended to come and kiss his master; in fact he brought a band of soldiers to arrest him (Matthew 26). We are almost as bad as Judas, because we come to Church pretending to serve and worship God, but we bring with us in our minds a gang of enemies to provoke and spite him.

HONOURING GOD BY GIVING

The second matter of honour is God's income. I'm talking about special gifts and bequests for the support of the work of his church. We must respect land and goods given freely for the work of God. We must respect the payment of his ministers. It is quite right that they should be paid, because by serving him in this calling they forfeit the opportunity of gaining a living in the world. The people under their pastoral care are obliged to support them. Paul says:

We have sown spiritual seed among you. Is it too much if we reap material benefits from you? (1 Corinthians 9.11)

Our ministers give us spiritual things, instruction, help towards attaining eternal life. Is it reasonable to begrudge them necessities of this life? If we avoid this duty it is like theft. Ministers have a right to their livelihood by the same law which gives all the rest of us a right to our property. We must support them; to do less is to rob God.

I ask you, is it right for a person to cheat God? Of course not, yet you are cheating me. 'How?' you ask. In the matter of tithes and offerings. (Malachi 3.8)

Whatever is set apart for God's purposes may not be used in any other way.

Watch out for the curse which comes on those who disobey this law. Long experience shows us that God punishes the mis-appropriation of goods dedicated to him. So if you want to hang on to your property don't ever tamper with anything set apart for God.

HONOURING GOD ON SUNDAY

Then there is the honouring of time. The Jews set apart the seventh day, the Sabbath. We Christians keep Sunday, the Lord's Day. The Jews commemorated the creation of the world; we celebrate the resurrection of Christ – the entry into a new world. This day is set apart for the worship and service of God: first publicly and with dignity, in the congregation. (And there is to be no staying away without good reason!) Then, privately at home – praying with our families and teaching them, or by ourselves in the privacy of our rooms; reading, thinking, praying. We are commanded to break from our everyday work in order to have the leisure for these things. But don't let's think that all God wants is for us to relax. When we stop work we have spiritual duties. The ordinance of the Lord's day was never a prescription for laziness! – Nor is our time free for indulgence in sins – many spend more time on Sundays eating and drinking than they do praying.

If we think of it, one day off a week is a great blessing. There is so much to do the rest of the week, and if there were no fixed time we probably would not stop at all. Then our souls would never eat – they would starve. Properly used, Sunday can bring us a regular diet – spiritual food to nourish eternal life in us. We are not to feel that Sunday is a waste of time, like the people of Amos' day:

> We can hardly wait for the holy days to be over so that we can sell our corn. When will the Sabbath end so that we can start selling again? (Amos 8.5)

We are to think of a day's break as a profitable time – the happiest day of the week. It is a spiritual shopping-day when we stock in food for a whole week. Some of the benefit will last us all our life.

In addition to the weekly Lord's Day there are other occasions on which the Church remembers God's special mercies – the birth and resurrection of Jesus Christ, the coming of the Holy Spirit, and so on. These must be kept as occasions of special thanksgiving. For us, who are so thankful for God's mercies, it can't be too much to spend a few days in the year saying 'thank you'! But we do have to make sure that such a feast is really spiritual. It is a holy day, not just a merry party. Christmas is more than good cheer and jollity;

it is for the the honour of Christ who came to bring all purity and
gentleness into the world. Don't let his coming be remembered in
any other way! And whatever days are set apart for honour,
memory, and celebration, we are to observe as our church directs
and benefit by them.

HONOURING GOD'S WORD

We express our reverence for God, too, by honouring his word.
The best way of slighting a person is to ignore what he says. If we
value someone's opinion we weigh his every word. God speaks to
us through the Holy Scriptures – the Old and the New Testaments.
In them he shows us his will and our duty. So we are to look upon
his word as the rule by which we live. We must read and study as
much as we can, if possible never letting a day pass without
reading the Bible or listening to a Bible passage.

But Bible study doesn't stop there: we must take in fully what we
are reading, storing it carefully in our memory – not letting it in one
ear and out the other. God's words must be so fixed in our minds
that we can think about them often. Then they can be ready for our
use. By them we shall plan and steer our lives. Then if we are
tempted to do something evil, we can call to mind the verse which
says God forbids it. And the Bible will tell us the consequences
of failure.

When we come across an opportunity to do good we can
remember: this is the very thing which the Bible said I should do.
Then how glorious are the rewards! So our Bible reading will
strengthen us to resist evil and to do good.

God speaks not only through the pages of the Bible, but through
his ministers who teach about him – not of course by saying
anything contrary to the scriptures, for that can't be right – but by
explaining it and making it easier to understand. Preachers apply
the Bible to our own particular circumstances and encourage us to
do well. So pay attention to what they say, because it concerns
you deeply.

Teaching is the laying of foundations upon which all Christian
practice must be built. Teaching is especially important to young
people. All children should be instructed so that they are not
ignorant when they get older. And it is up to the parents to make
sure that they learn. It is their responsibility and, if they fail, the
guilt is on their heads. Many parents sadly neglect this duty, so
that most people who call themselves Christians know little more
of Christ – or of anything that concerns their own souls – than does

any heathen. But though it is not your fault thay you were not instructed while you were young, now it is if you stay ignorant. Listen to this warning:

> You have never had any useful knowledge and have always refused to obey the Lord. You have never wanted my advice, or paid any attention when I corrected you. So then, you will get what you deserve, and your own actions will make you sick. Inexperienced people die because they reject wisdom. Stupid people are destroyed by their own lack of concern. But whoever listens to me will have security. He will be safe, with no reason to be afraid. (Proverbs 1.29)

For those who can build on well-laid foundations, preaching provides further help. Even if we know our duty well, we forget it or our own ideas blot it out. So it is very important that we should be reminded, encouraged, and helped to stand up to those things which would make us sin. Preaching warns us to be on our guard against our spiritual enemy. And it supplies us with weapons for the fight.

So we must not think that we have done our duty just by listening to a sermon – however carefully we have listened. We have to store the advice and apply it. It's not the prescription that makes you well – it's taking the medicine!

> Do not deceive yourselves by just listening to his word; instead, put it into practice. (James 1.22)

Don't measure your godliness by the number of sermons you hear! The hearing of sermons isn't the mark of a good Cristian, but the fruit that he bears in his life.

It's important to be discerning about preachers:

> My dear friends, do not believe all who claim to have the spirit, but test them to find out if the spirit they have comes from God. For many false prophets have gone out everywhere! (1 John 4.1)

We have to test the spirit of preaching to see if it comes from God. Preaching we can respect is the preaching of those who have a lawful calling to the task, and who expound the written word of God. And if you can't tell if the preaching reflects the word of God, then use your common sense of duty. Preaching that offers liberty to commit known sins is contrary to God and his word; it is abhorrent and must be rejected.

HONOURING GOD'S SACRAMENTS

God is honoured when we reverence his sacraments – baptism, and the Lord's supper. We must regard them highly as ways by which he blesses us.

Baptism brings us into 'covenant' with God – the divine contract. It makes us part of Christ, and so by right we get all the benefits that flow from him – forgiveness, his loving strength which makes us holy, and heaven itself. But we have to do our part in the covenant.

The Lord's supper is not only a symbol and a reminder of his death, but God uses it to bring Christ – and all we gain by his death – to everyone who takes part in the right spirit. We must value these sacraments most highly. How should we use them?

BAPTISM

We could not be expected to do much about our baptism if we received it when we were children, though we have great responsibility if we come to be baptised when we are grown up. If we were baptised as children, our Christian parents will have made promises for us; promises that when we grew up we would fulfil our part of the covenant. So what matters is our responsibility now.

If you want to know what these duties are, have a look at the promises which your godparents made in your name: they promised that you would:

> Fight valiantly under the banner of Christ against sin, the world, and the devil, and continue his faithful soldier and servant to the end of your life. (*The baptism service of the Church of England*).

By the fighting against the devil is meant rejecting everything we put in the place of God. Putting other things in God's place is like worshipping the devil. Idolatory was rife when Christ came to the world so that, when his followers were first told to baptise, rejecting false gods was made part of the promise. And although we don't make a religion out of idolatory now, it's still common enough! There are plenty of things we do which must be a great provocation to God. Remember how such provocations once led him to destroy whole cities with fire (Genesis 19), and the whole world with water (Genesis 6)! Idolatory still brings down judgement on those who practise it.

One of the baptism promises is not to have any dealings with the devil – witchcraft or spiritism of any sort – for whatever reason. To some extent this too is idolatory because it means leaving God and setting up the devil for our God, going to him for help.

We promise in baptism that we will have nothing to do with the works of the devil.

From the very beginning he was a murderer and has never been on the side of truth, because there is no truth in him. When he tells a lie, he is only doing what is natural to him, because he is a liar and the father of all lies. (John 8.44)

We never become so like the devil as when we incite others to sin, for that's the devil's own profession.

Another baptism promise is to reject the superficial pride and preoccupation of the world around us. To us this means rejecting all that goes to excess - eating, entertainment, dress etc. Then there are the temptations of our own jobs and circumstances to be resisted, the lure of money and power. That is not to say that a Christian shouldn't be rich or powerful, but our emotions and affections and our energies shouldn't be totally bound up in this way. And we shouldn't try to get or keep wealth or power by unlawful means. However delightful the company of our friends, we mustn't be trapped by them into doing wrong. Nor should we accept just any fashion or tradition. It's better to be thought odd and silly and to be isolated for it, than to join a crowd on the way to hell.

And we renounce sin at baptism.

The acts of the sinful nature are obvious: sexual immorality, impurity and debauchery; idolatory and witchcraft; hatred, discord, jealousy, fits of rage, selfish ambition, dissensions, factions and envy; drunkenness, orgies, and the like. (Galatians 5.19-21)

This is just one of the descriptions that occur throughout the scriptures. We promised to forsake these things.

If we were baptised as children, our parents and Godparents promised belief in the Christian faith, expressed in what we call the 'Creed'. And we are supposed to learn these things – not only the words, but also the meaning; not only to learn them, but to live by them. For example, we believe that God created us, so we should live in obedience to him as creator. We believe that Christ redeemed us, so we should let him have what he has bought back – ourselves, to be directed by him and employed in his service. We believe in his Holy Spirit, so we should let him fill our lives.

We are told in baptism that we must continue as God's faithful soldiers and servants to the end of our lives. So we have to do what he has told us to do in the Bible, and to go on obeying him every day of our life – not a few steps into his way, but a long walk; not for part of our time, but all day, every day, as long as we live in this world.

The promises of baptism are made to God. But don't forget that we need to keep them for our own benefit. I mentioned the covenant-agreement with God into which baptism brings us. Now there are two sides to an agreement. If one party breaks his side of it, he can't reasonably expect the other party to keep his. It's just the same with the covenant of baptism: there's no reason why God should be tied to keeping his promises if we don't keep ours. But supposing we do break our promises? Without the covenant, we are left as God found us. And what can make up for losing God's favour and grace? What can make up for losing our souls for ever?

'Does a person gain anything if he wins the whole world but loses his life?' said Jesus. (Mark 8.36)

So, when we are tempted to sin our thought should not be 'It's only a little one' (Genesis 19.20). We have to remember what was promised through baptism. Then we shall know that however little is the sin, it has great implications. For by doing it we break our agreement with God.

THE LORD'S SUPPER

Before he comes to communion,

'Everyone should examine himself first, and then
eat the bread and drink from the cup'.
(1 Corinthians 11.28)

What we are doing in the Lord's supper is to repeat and renew that agreement made with God in our baptism. We know that we have sadly broken it in many ways. God is kind, and he lets us renew it in this sacrament of communion. If we come sincerely and in faith, he has promised to accept us. Here he will renew every blessing which would have been ours from baptism if only we had not failed him.

Do you understand what the covenant idea is all about? If you don't it's important that you find someone to tell you about it. It may be of help for you to look again at the pages about 'The Second Covenant' in our introduction. It's really wrong that you should go on coming to the Lord's table not really knowing what you are doing.

What about examining our consciences before we come? The best way of doing this is to check our actions against God's law. Don't be content with the general knowledge that you have broken it, but try to think in what ways you have done so. Think, as fully as you can, of the various periods of your life. In each of them remember where you have gone wrong – I don't just mean gross acts of sin, but words and secret thoughts. For though there's no State law against thoughts, there are divine laws. Wherever God forbids the act, he forbids the thought – the desire to do it. Evil thoughts are just as clear to him as the most public misdemeanour. Don't forget that God expects you to reject your sins and to confess them when you come to ask for forgiveness. We can't confess things that we've put out of our minds, and we can't resolve to turn our back on sins that we are not aware of. That's why this self-examination is so important. We must make a strict search of our hearts and our minds. Search your soul through and through that it may be entirely healed.

Just let's see how devious our sins are. There's consciously sinning; when we know a thing to be wrong but we do it for pleasure, profit or just adventure. There's sinning deliberately; after thinking about it. Worse still, there's repeating a sin again and again – every time it's worse. When people keep on hurting us in the same way, we find it less forgivable each time. What about the way we repeatedly sin against God?

Worst of all is becoming hardened to our sin – we get so used to it that we just don't know what we are doing. Then we are in great danger. We can come to love the sin, not only in ourselves but in others. We...

not only continue to do these things, but even approve of others who do them. (Romans 1.32)

Now the point of this examination before we approach the Lord's table is to make us humble. We need to realise how sinful we are to make us sensitive to our own danger – the danger of coming before the majesty of God when we have provoked him so terribly. Again, the examination is to make us sorry for our sin, sorry that we've been so ungrateful. We have offended a good and gracious God. We have been unkind in return for his tender mercy.

Let us be as sad and penitent as our sins have been great. This sense of unworthiness will be acceptable to God who does not 'reject a humble and repentant heart' (Psalm 51.17). And it's likely our sorrow will also help us to reform, for once we have felt the

wounds of sorrow, we shall be less keen to start sinning all over
again.

Whatever we do we must not be sorry for ourselves; the sadness
must be a genuine regret for our failure. Sorrow before God is
genuine when it is joined with love. Then we grieve for having hurt
him even if there is no prospect of punishment. If we want to be
genuinely sorry, we must remind ourselves of the many good
things that he has done for us – not least that he has refrained from
destroying us for our sin! We should be ashamed and angry at
ourselves for being so ungrateful to him.

Our self-examination needs to be done in the framework of
prayer. As we pray, we look at Jesus, whom God has

> offered so that by his death he should become the means by
> which people's sins are forgiven through their faith in him...the
> lamb of God who takes away the sins of the world! (Romans
> 3.25, John 1.29)

And we must plead with God from our hearts that through Christ's
blood our sins may be cleansed away, and God, for his sake, may
become our friend again. We can be sure that if we leave our sins
and truly give ourselves to God, obeying his commands, this will
really happen.

Our resolutions at the Lord's table must be sincere. It is wrong
to come without a sincere hatred of our sins, and with no intention
of keeping our promises afterwards. Don't let's deceive ourselves,
God knows our hearts. We can't hide anything from him, and we
are in great danger if we try.

It is worth giving some thought to the ways in which we have
fallen into sin and what has brought us to it; where, and when, and
in what company it happened. Then we can guard ourselves
against repeating it by keeping away from that situation.

The time to reject any particular sin is before you come to the
Lord's table; it's not good enough to intend to break with it
afterwards. Get an immediate divorce from your old beloved sins,
or you are in no way fit to be married to Christ. Sin is death and the
sacrament is spiritual food. Nobody feeds a dead person! Paul says
we can 'bring judgement on ourselves as we eat and drink'
(1 Corinthians 11.29).

Jesus said,

> When an evil spirit goes out of a person, it travels over dry
> country looking for a place to rest. If it can't find one it says to

itself 'I will go back to my house'. So it goes back and finds the house clean and tidy. Then it goes out and brings seven other spirits even worse than itself, and they come and live there. So when it is all over, that person is in a worse state than he was at the beginning. (Luke 11.24-26)

Remember this, and when you rid yourselves from sin's occupation, open yourself to the gifts of Christ. By prayer invite the Holy Spirit to fill you with the qualities he brings.

When we come to the Lord's table, we must copy his most perfect example and forgive others who have offended us. And don't let's stop there, but show kindness, and the service of love and friendship to them. It may be that you forgot Jesus' example of forgiveness, and were unkind or hurt someone. Now is the chance to go and say sorry and to ask his forgiveness. Acknowledge that you were in the wrong and give him back anything that you have taken from him. It is absolutely necessary to do this before we come to God, or he cannot accept our worship. Christ says,

If you are about to offer your gift to God at the altar and there you remember that your brother has something against you, leave your gift there in front of the altar. Go at once and make peace with your brother, and then come back and offer your gift to God. (Matthew 5.23,24)

Coming with others to the Lord's table declares our brotherly love and charity, and it's sheer hypocrisy if we come with any malice in our hearts.

When you come to the Lord's supper, set aside the things which preoccupy you in your daily life. Be 'devoted' to him. A special part of your devotion will be prayer – frequent, and very sincere; because prayer is the way to be prepared. If you try and make yourself fit for God's presence in your own strength, you will never do it. He alone can make us ready, so we need to pray to him.

We are not good enough in ourselves to have a high estimate of ourselves, but any ability we have comes from God. (2 Corinthians 3.5)

Therefore go straight away to him to help you. He will make you fit for his table, so that you can enjoy all the blessings which he gives.

Do you remember Jesus' story of the wedding clothes?

The king went in to look at the guests and saw a man who was not wearing wedding clothes. 'Friend, how did you get in here without wedding clothes?' the king asked him. But the man said

nothing. Then the king told the servants, 'Tie him up hand and
foot, and throw him outside in the dark. There he will cry and
grind his teeth'. (Matthew 22.11-13)

So it is with us when we come thoughtlessly and carelessly to the
Lord's table.

There's just one thing to add: don't rely altogether on your own
opinion as to how prepared you are. For humble souls sometimes
judge themselves too harshly, while others make too favourable an
estimate. So if it's possible that you might be mistaken in either
way take the advice that the church has always given; go to a
'discreet and godly minister'. He will be able to make an objective
assessment and give unprejudiced advice. Many run into trouble
because they won't accept this suggestion; they get depressed by
their sense of unworthiness and their conscience is deeply distressed.
Or, worse, some have tried to blot out their failure by an excess of
sinful pleasure.

You can't confess your sin to someone else without finding out
how truly naked and scarred is your soul. That is what puts people
off doing it. But it is an unreasonable and unfortunate attitude and
it shouldn't stop you. On the other hand you do need to choose
someone who will faithfully keep any secret you will give him. If he
is a godly man, he won't think any the worse of you for telling him
your failure. In fact he'll gain a better opinion because you are
obviously keen to set things right between God and yourself. Don't
feel any shame in confession for, given godly counsel, it will help
you find a cure for your trouble and sin. The man who misses a cure
by preferring not to discover what's wrong with mis is a fool. If we
do the same for our souls, we are all the more foolish, as the soul is
so much more precious than the body.

But God knows, it's not only diffident peopole who need pastoral
counselling, but the complacent even more so. Somebody else's
assessment would do them a lot of good. On the whole we tend to
have too high an estimate of ourselves, and it's good to be advised
by a spiritual guide so that we can get things into perspective.
What's more, we may gain some advice on how to control our
inclinations to sin.

Honouring God at his table

When you come to God's table first be humble. Acknowledge that
you don't deserve to be there. And remember just between God
and you, some of the worst things you've done and how you have
broken the promises made last time you came. Then think how

Jesus suffered. When you see the bread broken, remember how he was put on the cross – his body torn with nails. When you see the wine poured out, remember him bleeding there. And think of your sins as causing both his shattered body and his spilt blood. What a thing to have done – to have given him such pain! Aren't you worse than those who crucified him? They crucified him once; but you, in a sense, have crucified him daily. They crucified him because they didn't know him, but you knew who he was – the Lord of Glory. To you he has been a kind and loving Saviour; and yet you have crucified him again and again. Think of this and let it make you deeply sorry for your past sins, and stir up in you a great hatred of them and a determination not to sin again.

Now think of Jesus' sufferings in a different way. Let them strengthen your faith. Look on Jesus as the sacrifice offered for your sins – that God may not condemn you, that he may be merciful and kind towards you. And pray to God – asking humbly, but believing, that he will accept the sacrifice of his dear Son to cover whatever you have done wrong and to pardon you; asking him to be reconciled to you.

Now let Christ's pain and agony make you thankful to him. Remember his bitter cry, 'My God, my God, why did you abandon me?' (Matthew 27.46)

Christ suffered all this to keep you from disaster. How much you have to thank him for! Be enthusiastically grateful. Praise and glorify the loving-kindness which has bought us back for God, at such cost.

What can I offer the Lord
   for all his goodness to me?
I will bring a wine offering to the Lord,
   to thank him for saving me.
In the assembly of all his people
   I will give him what I have promised...
I will give you a sacrifice of thanksgiving
   and offer my prayer to you.
In the assembly of all your people,
   in the sanctuary of your temple in Jerusalem
I will give you what I have promised.
   Praise the Lord!

(Psalm 116.12-14, 17-19)

Let Christ's suffering engender love in your heart. And no better way can it be done that in thinking about the cross, for by the cross, the love of Christ is most obviously shown.

This is how we know what love is: Christ gave his life for us. (John 3.16)

The greatest love a person can have for his friends is to give his life for them. (John 15.13)

And his love was greater yet – it wasn't shown just in his dying, but in a death most painful and most shameful. It wasn't a love just for his friend, but for his sworn enemies too. If after all this love of his there is no return of love on our part, aren't we worse than the worst sort of people? Scold yourself because your love is so weak and cold, while his for you is so persevering and deep. And try to kindle this fire of love in your soul; to love him so much that you are ready to take his example – to part with everything when he asks you, yes even life itself. And beg him to help you put your sins to death.

Just before you accept the consecrated bread and wine, remember that this is God, sealing his agreement with you – his new covenant made for mankind through his Son. For just as the Lord comes to us in this Supper, so he brings with him all the blessing of the covenant. These blessings are: a pardon for sin, love and strength to help us lead a holy life, and the right to life eternal. Marvel, then, at the goodness of God who gives to us his Son.

As soon as you have received the bread and wine, give devoted praise to God for his great love and kindness, and pray for God's Spirit to help you keep the promises you have now made.

After communion

Christ is the sacrifice before God for our sins – through whom we may be forgiven – and not our sins only, but the sins of everyone. (1 John 2.2)

So let your love reach out as far as his has done, and pray for all mankind, that everyone may know the blessing of that sacrifice of his. Pray for the life of the church – especially your own congregation. Pray for those whom you honour and obey both in church and State. Pray for those who are close to you and those who are in need. If there is a collection – there should always be a collection for the poor at the Lord's Supper – give as much as you can afford. If they leave the collection out, personally give something to those who are not so well off as you. And make sure to take the next opportunity of giving it. It's best to do all this while other people are receiving their communion, so that when the prayers of the congregation begin, you may be ready to join in.

Don't go straight from the the Lord's Supper to involvement in every-day affairs. There's more thinking, praying and reading to be done, and useful conversation to be entered into. These things will keep alight the divine flame burning in your heart. And when you do get down to work again, remember that you have a still more important work to do: all that you promised to God so recently. Remember everything you said to him, and set your heart on doing it. When the same old temptations come, remember how determined you were not to give in – remember how very guilty you will feel if you do! For when you received the bread and wine, God and you entered into a covenant, an agreement of friendship and kindness. As long as you keep in that friendship with God, you are safe: neither man nor devil can hurt you.

If you do give into temptation, you will find an additional enemy – your own conscience, accusing you. And being against God and your own conscience at one and the same time is a desperate situation.

Don't let God's kindness in forgiving you in the past encourage you to sin again!

Don't despise his great kindness, tolerance and patience. Surely you know that God is kind, because he is trying to lead you to repent. (Romans 2.3)

Let me say this: the more often you have been forgiven, the less reason you have to expect forgiveness again; because your sin becomes worse after God has been so kind. Walking with Christ should make keeping free from sin that much easier. So that when you are an experienced Christian, failure is more culpable.

Even though our promises made at the Lord's Supper are for life, we should renew them often. In other words, we should come often to his table because God blesses us there, and because Christ commands it:

'Do this in remembrance of me.'
(1 Corinthians 11.24)

So both logically and out of duty we need to come often to his holy table.

HONOURING GOD'S NAME

What is meant by 'honouring God's name'? Let's look at it the other way round: How might God's name be *dis*honoured?

First, by blasphemy. Blasphemy is saying anything evil about God, the worst blasphemy being to curse him. Blasphemies are not just spoken – God also knows our hearts and sees what we are thinking. And things we do can be blasphemy; for instance, if we get an evil reputation as the servants of God and it reflects badly upon him. Paul saw this happening with the Jews:

> The Scripture says, 'Because of you Jews, the Gentiles speak evil of God.' (Romans 2.24)

Then there's swearing. Here are the pitfalls:

1. I might swear that somebody did something when I know that it's not true – that's perjury.

2. It's perjury if I swear something is true when I don't really know it is.

3. However well-intentioned I might be when I swear to do something, if I don't do what I vowed to do, that also becomes perjury.

4. Be careful that oaths you swear don't contradict each other! If they do, you have to break one or the other of them.

Now let's look at the nature of false swearing. We call on God to witness the truth of our oaths. If what we say is false, it is a direct affront to God. For it suggests either that we think that we can deceive him – and that makes him less than all-knowing; or that he is willing to countenance our lies – which makes him a party to them. One way we make him too ignorant to be God, and the other way we make him a liar like the devil, the father of liars (John 8.44). Either way God's name is dishonoured. He says,

> Do not use my name for evil purposes, for I, the Lord your God, will punish anyone who misuses my name. (Exodus 20.7; Deuteronomy 5.11)

If you want to know more about the curses that fall on those who tell lies under oath, read Zechariah 5.1-5. You will find that when the punishment comes it affects family, house and property. How important it is – for time and eternity – to guard against this sin!

Another type of false swearing is to use God's name for silly oaths. Jesus said,

> Do not swear at all: either by heaven, for it is God's throne; or by the earth, for it is his footstool. (Matthew 5.34,35)

Careless and empty promises are fashionable, but when God judges us and we have to answer for bringing his name into disrepute, he won't accept the excuse 'everybody was doing it'. We'll be all the more guilty, because by joining them we helped to establish the fashion. We should have tried to stop it and shown disapproval.

It's not only that by much swearing we disobey Christ's instructions, it's that we trivialise reference to God. If we swear on oath, we are asking God to judge the truth of what we say. God is great and majestic, and to appeal to him implies that the matter is of great weight and importance; that his own glory is at stake, or at least we are deeply concerned with the good of mankind. But if we swear in the course of normal conversation (and for some, every other sentence has an oath), we despise him. We call God, the great king of the world, to witness our childish and trivial concerns.

With swearing, much use is the path to misuse. If you swear often, you are all the more likely to take a dreadful oath without thinking about it. If you don't notice what you are swearing to, you're far more likely to lie; you are prepared to swear the truth of anything without consideration. So you are going to perjure yourself often in the sight of God.

The strange thing is that there is no satisfaction to be gained by this sin. We give the devil everything and he doesn't give us anything in return. Why then, do people swear? I think it is because they hope to gain credibility; the more they swear the more they think people will believe them. The truth is quite the reverse; the frequent swearer is the last to be believed. And for good reason, for whoever has no conscience about profaning God's name is unlikely to have much conscience about lying. When people support everything they say with an oath, it looks as if they're covering something up! So swearing doesn't serve them well at all. And since there's nothing to be gained from it, there's no excuse for it. To hurt God like this without any provocation is contemptuous and unloving.

You might imagine that the sin is a small one since it's so common. Yet it's far from being small, either in its own right, or from God's point of view.

So if you haven't yet fallen into the habit of swearing, be very careful not to start. If it's already trapped you, get out as you love your soul. And don't tell me that it's a hard habit to break – that's no excuse. The longer you've been doing it the more reason you have to stop quickly – you've been doing it long enough! If you practise the habit much longer you may find is impossible to break.

How then can we break this habit? First, realise how sinful it is. Take notice of the easy attitude of the world. Then, think of the dangers: it puts you out of favour with God and, if you go on with it, puts you into hell for ever. If somebody tells me that he's finding it difficult to break the habit, I ask him if he could break it if he were sure that he'd be hanged the next time he swore an oath. Under those circumstances, any man in his right mind would master himself. Surely damnation is *worse* than hanging? The truth is that people don't think this sin will damn them – or at least they think that the Judgement is such a long way off that it's not too great a worry. But that's illogical: everyone who wilfully continues in sin is asking for damnation. And how do you know that you won't die with the false oath on your lips? Besides, eternal damnation, however far off it may be, is still fearful. Here are the ways to avoid the pitfall of swearing:

1. Practise being strictly correct in all you say, so that people may believe you on your word alone, then you won't need an oath to make it credible.

2. Note what most leads you into this sin. Is it drink? Losing your temper? The company you keep? The example of others? What is it? If you're serious about the sin, you'll keep away from the opportunities.

3. Keep your heart reverent always towards God. If this becomes a habit it will soon displace profanity. Get the habit of respect for God, and particularly for his name. Never mention it without praise in your heart, even in normal conversation.

4. If you use God's name, make it an opportunity to think of him with love. Keep it out of careless conversation.

5. Watch yourself constantly: 'Lord, place a guard at my mouth, a sentry at the door of my lips' (Psalm 141.3).

If you try and overcome this habit, God will help you. I have spent time on this, because it is a sin that is so prevalent at the moment.

May God in his mercy show people who are guilty of it how very wrong it is!

So by understanding how we may dishonour God's name, we see how to honour it:

Everyone will praise his great and majestic name. Holy is he! (Psalm 99.3)

PRAYER

Worship belongs to God alone – hence its importance. To worship, our soul contributes prayer. Here are the forms of prayer:

Confession is the acknowledging of our sins to God. Whenever we pray, publicly or privately, we confess our general sinfulness. But we should confess particular sins – incidents which we know to be sinful – regularly, and often. We should express our sorrow daily in our private prayer. Remember that our confession is not intended to instruct God – he knows our sins much better than we do. But confession brings humility, and until we are really humble before God, we have not finished confessing.

Petition is asking God for the specific needs of our souls and bodies. For our souls we ask forgiveness for Jesus' sake. To bring us forgiveness he has shed his blood. And we ask for the help of God's Spirit to enable us to let go our sins and to obey him all the time. We need to ask specifically for virtues like faith, love, enthusiasm, holiness, sorrow for sin etc. – especially for the things we most lack.

So discover what your needs are: if you are proud, pray for humility; if you are evil-minded, for purity, and so for every other gift of God – just as you need to be strengthened. If it's for the good of your soul, be persistent about praying. Don't take 'no' for an answer, or give up, even if for the time you don't get what you ask for. No matter how long you've been asking God for something like this, don't give up praying! Find out what stops your prayers being answered. Perhaps you're asking for strength to overcome some sin, and yet you have never lifted a finger to do anything about it – in fact you have gone out of your way to look for temptation. No wonder your prayers aren't answered. You won't let them be! Put it right. Do your part and you can be sure that God will do his.

As regards our physical wants, we are to ask God to give us things that we need for our life here on earth; but to leave to his wisdom how much he gives us. We should not expect to choose the best for ourselves, praying for everything we might set our hearts on. We can only pray for things that will help us to glorify him and to keep our souls safe from danger.

Then we should pray that God will help us to overcome our weaknesses. This is a daily duty – most especially when temptation threatens. We must cry out for God's help, like Peter when he began to sink in the water:

'Save me, Lord!' (Matthew 14.30)

We can ask that God save us from anything that might hurt us, though we need to tell him that we are happy with whatever he sends as long as his will is done:

My Father, if it is possible, take this cup of suffering from me. Yet not what I want, but what you want. (Matthew 26.39)

Intercession is praying for others. We must do this for everybody – strangers as well as friends. We have special obligations to pray for those who lead us in church or State, and for our close relatives. We are told to pray for all who are ill or in trouble, and those whom we believe to be in special danger. There is no distinction to be made; we must pray for those who hurt us as well as those we love.

But now I tell you…love your enemies and pray for those who persecute you, so that you may become the sons of your Father in Heaven. (Matthew 5.44,45)

Jesus gives us the highest example, praying on the cross for his enemies:

Forgive them, Father! they don't know what they are doing. (Luke 23.34)

Prayers of *thanksgiving* offer praises to God for all his love and kindness – to ourselves, to our church and nation, and to all mankind. We thank him for his goodness both spiritual and material. We thank him for giving his Son, for sending his Spirit, and every way he has used to bring ordinary men and women back to himself. Then we thank him for his goodness to us individually; that we have been brought up in the family of the church, taught the Christian faith; that we have benefited by his word and sacraments; that without effort on our part we have been offered the way to eternal life.

And there is not one of us who hasn't received extra spiritual blessings from God for which we should thank him. There's God's patience with us: waiting for our repentance and not damning us straight away. There God's counselling: it comes outwardly when he speaks to us through the Bible and through preaching; and it comes inwardly by the voice of his Spirit. If by God's grace you have been drawn by his voice, and brought from a life of disregard for God into the Christian way, surely you more than any one are bound to praise him for his goodness! You have received the greatest of gifts.

We must thank God for material blessings: that the church can flourish in our land; that our land is free and peaceful; for the good things of this life which we enjoy – health, friendship, food, clothes etc. We must thank him for his many blessings every day: he keeps us from danger. It would be impossible to detail everything which any one of you might have received from God, because experiences are so different. But we can be sure of this: that the one who is given the least still receives enough to spend his whole life praising God. I suggest you think back over your life, making a list of the great things God has done for you. Make a list, memorise them, and often thank God for them.

Every aspect of prayer is to be used publicly and privately. When we are in church we unite in prayer because we have a common concern. We must pray in church regularly because Christ promises special blessings to those who join together in prayer. If you stay away without good reason you cut yourself off from the church, which is an extremely serious matter.

Then there are family prayers. This is the first responsibility of the father of the household. It is just as important that he provides food for his chilren's souls as for their bodies. How to go about it? If you can read, you can always use a good book of prayers. One good choice would be the church service book. Even if you can't read, it's good to have some prayers which you can say together, and church prayers are very suitable because they are easy to memorise; they are short but contain a good deal. But whatever your choice, make sure that you do pray. Don't let anyone who says he is a Christian lead his family into a heathen lack of worship. He must see that God is worshipped in the family – daily.

Private or secret prayers we use when we are on our own. In these we can be far more specific than is proper in public. But public worship doesn't let us out of praying privately. Both are needed, and they are not interchangeable. Remember what Jesus said about those who are good at praying in public but don't bother in private; they want to impress others, but they don't impress God (Matthew 6). It's God we are praying to, and it is his reward we are looking for, not the shallow praises of other people.

Pray in private morning and evening – not less frequently. Prayer is the way we should begin and end all our work, not only because it is our duty to God, but because we can't prosper without him, or remain safe unless we ask for his protection. We should be afraid to embark on a day or night except in his safe-keeping.

How much more than this we might pray privately to God would depend on our occupation. Some jobs leave moments for prayers and others do not. But even if we are very short of time, we can lift up our hearts to him even while we are working. The more leisure we have, the more reason we have to give more time to prayer. And don't let anybody who has time for pleasure (time even for sin!) say that they haven't time for praying. If we knew how much we had to gain from prayer we would think it wise to be as frequent in prayer as we are infrequent now.

Do we realise what an honour it is for us, worms that we are, to be able to speak so freely to the king of heaven? If we were given the opportunity to speak to a head of state we should be the envy of our neighbours, and it's scarcely likely that we should refuse the opportunity. But that is nothing to the honour conferred on those who can speak to God. We ought to grab at the chance.

And how we can benefit ourselves by praying! Through prayer comes everything good for body and soul. If we pray right and humbly the answer is certain:

> The prayer of the humble pierces the clouds, but he is not consoled until it reaches its destination. He does not desist until the Most High intervenes, gives the just their rights, and sees justice done. (Ecclesiasticus 35.17)

You would think that with this prospect we would all pray no matter how much trouble it was. In fact this duty is far from hard, and being in the presence of God is very pleasant.

> You have made known to me the path of life; you will fill me with joy in your presence, with eternal pleasures at your right hand. (Psalm 17.11)

So the nearer we draw to God, the happier we are. To be close to him is heaven. Prayer is the way of drawing close to him in this life. If it is able to give us so much delight and pleasure, isn't there something wrong with us if we can't face it? The truth is this: prayer is a pleasant duty, but it's a spiritual one. So if your heart is unspiritual, if it's set on a course of physical pleasure, it's hardly surprising if you don't feel like praying. Compare the Israelites, who despised the bread that they were given in the desert, because they hankered after the scraps of meat they had as slaves in Egypt. So if you find prayer a burden, suspect that there may be something wrong in you, expel the love of sin from your heart! Try to bring yourself to a more spiritual state, and you will find your praying delightful and satisfying. Meanwhile don't complain about prayer being difficult, but about your own attitude being unworthy.

Of course it may be lack of practice. Like anything else, praying is going to get easier the more often you do it. Though it's not just how often we pray, but how well we pray. Never should we ask for anything that's unlawful, like revenge on our enemies. Always we should ask in faith, believing either that he'll give us what we ask or else he's planning something that is better for us. We must approach God humbly, knowing ourselves to be quite unworthy of the things we're asking for – that's why we can ask only 'for Jesus Christ's sake'.

We should concentrate on what we are saying. Prayer may be the work of the soul but, if our minds wander, it's all chatter as far as God is concerned. How foolish it is that we come to God with such important matters and let our minds wander! Imagine a criminal coming before a judge to appeal against a death sentence: he spots a butterfly out of the corner of his eye and decides to chase it around the dock. Do you think the judge could take his appeal seriously? And how do we expect God to grant our requests if we are not bothered about them ourselves?

If it is worrying us that our mind wanders in prayer, we need to come to our prayers with a consciousness of the majesty of the God we are approaching. We need a great concern for the things we are asking, and to think of the consequences of our not being heard. Our first prayer might be for God's help to keep our attention fixed.

If wanton thoughts do intrude, throw them out in disgust straight away, and ask God's pardon; if you apply yourself to the fight, either God will help you to some extent to defeat them or he will forgive what you can't help. But as long as you remain careless, you have no right to expect either.

Then, we must pray sincerely and with enthusiasm. We must give God the love and devotion of our souls. Cold and feeble requests are not going to impress God – they don't impress us! If someone asked us for help, and did it in such a cynical way that he didn't appear to care whether we help him or not, we should think he didn't need our help, or didn't really want it. Naturally we would feel disinclined to help him. The things we ask from God are so much more important than anything we could be asked for. So they should never be the subject of careless and superficial prayers. In the same way our praise and thanksgiving will hardly be accepted by God if it's not sincere and aware of his mercy to us. He's not going to accept from us mere compliments - he wants heartfelt thanks.

When you draw near to God in prayer you need to come with the highest enthusiasm and the deepest sincerity. Because you can't of yourself feel like this, you must ask God to set your heart on fire with devotion. And don't put the fire out again with any deliberate sin, or let it die for lack of use!

Paul says to Timothy:

I want men everywhere to lift up holy hands in prayer, without anger or disputing. (1 Timothy 2.8)

We must clear out from our hearts every tendency to sin, and especially arguments. If we don't, we can't lift up holy hands; and then our prayers - however long and earnest they are - won't get anywhere. The writer of the Psalms tells us that we just won't be heard:

If I ignore my sins the Lord will not listen to me. (Psalm 66.18)

In fact if we do wrong our prayers recoil on our own heads:

The Lord is pleased when good men pray but hates the sacrifices that wicked men bring him. (Proverbs 15.8)

Finally, we must pray for the right reasons, and the right things. We must not pray to make people admire us or just because we like to do as others do. We should pray to worship God, to acknowledge that he is the only source of blessings, and to gain from him the answers to our own and others' needs. The things we pray for must not be selfish: the end in view must be God's glory first; our salvation and the salvation of others next. Everything else we ask for must depend on these.

What about the outward expression of our worship? We need nothing more than a humble and reverent demeanour as we approach God. We are commanded to glorify God with our souls and our bodies; we must reverence him with both, for he has created and redeemed both. So let your prayers to God be with humility of body and mind:

> Come, let us bow down and worship him; let us kneel before the Lord our maker! (Psalm 95.6)

REPENTANCE

Repentance is simply turning away from sin and turning towards God. It is giving up what we used to do and doing what God requires of us as Christians.

If you keep an account of your expenses you'll know that it is much better to write them down every day and have a set period for keeping a balance, than to let the figures get out of hand. So we should keep short accounts with God, regularly humbling ourselves before him in penitence. If we don't, we run up such a long debt that we can't cope with it. I would say mark one day every week as the day when you do this and express your sorrow to him.

And there are other times when you might be prompted to repent. When troubles happen to you, you might look on them as a message from God to bring you to repentance:

> My son, pay attention when the Lord corrects you and do not be discouraged when he rebukes you. Because the Lord corrects everyone he loves, and punishes everyone he accepts as a son. (Hebrews 12.5,6)

There's another time of repentance – a custom which has slipped away – repentance when we are dying. It's a very good time to renew our repentance, but not a good time to start! And it's madness, and a terrible risk, that people leave repentance until then. How do you know you are going to have that last chance to repent when you are dying? Haven't you seen death come suddenly? How do you know that it won't happen to you? And even supposing illness gives you good warning, you might not take it in, and convince yourself – as often people do with terminal illness – that you are not dying. So that even if death comes very slowly you might not be prepared for it. And supposing you do see the danger, are you sure that you will be able to repent?

Repentance is given by God. We can't summon it up. And when we've resisted God's love for such a long time, he may well give us up to the hardness of our own hearts – and quite rightly.

Supposing God in his infinite patience once again affords you the opportunity to repent. You have been resisting it maybe thirty, forty or fifty years. It's become a habit to you. How do you know you can change your habit suddenly and make use of the opportunity he gives you? It's much easier for you to repent now than then. For one thing, the longer sin has kept hold on your heart, the harder it is to get rid of it. True the death bed is the best place for stopping sin, if that were all that there was to repentance (it's hard to commit sin in that situation!). But, as I've said, repentance is much more than this. It involves a sincere hatred of sin, and a love for God. And you can't change your affections quite so suddenly. Besides, don't forget that when you are ill it's very difficult to think of anything that needs concentration; repentance needs all our energies when we are fresh.

Be reasonable: what hope is there that you will do then what is more easy to do now? Don't forget that death-bed repentance may not be genuine. The fear of hell is not a bad thing when there is time to react to it properly. But on its own can never bring salvation. Too often people who repented because they thought they were dying have reverted to the careless lives they lived before, when God has been good enough to give them back their health. Obviously there was no real change in them at all. If someone dies with that sort of repentance, God is hardly likely to accept it; for he who tests our hearts can see our insincerity. When you consider these dangers put together, it's quite obviously reckless for anyone to rely on a death-bed repentance.

There was of course the case of the repentant thief who died next to Jesus on the cross (Luke 23.43). But there is a great difference betwen our situation and his; he had never heard of Christ before that, and took his first chance to receive him. But Christ has been offered to us – even pushed at us – since we were children, and still we turn him down. Listen to wisdom:

> Remember your Creator while you are still young, before those dismal days and years come when you will say, 'I don't enjoy life.' (Ecclesiastes 12.1)

The Old Testament usually puts repentance and fasting together. Among the Jews, the great day of atonement was to be kept with fasting (Leviticus 16.31, Isaiah 58.5). God directed that when the prophets called upon people to repent and be humble, they should also require fasting. For instance,

> But even now, says the Lord, repent sincerely and return to me with fasting and weeping and mourning. (Joel 2.12)

Fasting is not less appropriate since Christ came than it was before. We find him accepting it as a duty that must be performed sometimes, when he gives instructions to avoid pride:

> And when you fast, do not put on a sad face as the hypocrites do. They neglect their appearance so that everyone will see that they are fasting. I assure you, they have already been paid in full. When you go without food wash your face, and comb your hair, so that others cannot know that you are fasting – only your father, who is unseen, will know. And your father, who sees what you do in private, will reward you. (Matthew 6.18-18)

The saints practised fasting: Anna, for instance, in Luke 2.37. The early Christians practised it often.

In fact, fasting is not only limited to times of humble repentance, but is appropriate to times when we have something special to ask from God. When Esther was about to make an attempt to save her people, she and all the Jews kept a solemn fast (Esther 4.16). When Paul and Barnabas were to be made apostles, there was fasting and prayer (Acts 13.3). So when we need any special guidance or help from God, whether in respect of our material or our spiritual concerns, it's right to sharpen our prayers by fasting.

But fasting is a special part of making ourselves humble. By denying ourselves food, we discipline ourselves for eating too much in the past or for other over-indulgences, and we express a proper indignation that every sinner ought to have against his own selfishness. Anyone who is so soft on himself that he can't miss a single meal for discipline's sake shows that he is not too worried about his sin.

Though much self-denial is acceptable to God, yet we mustn't get the idea that it can make up for our wrong-doing; nothing but the blood of Christ can do that. So we must depend on him and not on what we do, for our forgiveness. Yet since his blood only avails for sinners who are penitent we should be as concerned to show our repentance, as if our hope depended on that alone.

How often should we fast? The Bible doesn't say. There are various factors – health and other considerations. But the more often we make ourselves humble the better. The more often we fast the more we get used to it and the less detrimental it will be to health and work. In addition fasting may give us greater opportunity for devotion because we can better employ the time we would otherwise spend eating.

2

Our Duty to Ourselves

God has revealed his grace for the salvation of all mankind. That grace instructs us to give up ungodly living and wordly passions and to live self-controlled, upright and godly lives in this world. (Titus 2.11)

I want to talk to you about this self-control, about upright living, and the virtues that characterise godly lives.

HUMILITY

Everything is built on humility. Humility is of first importance. Unless we build on humility, all our other virtues will collapse. We've talked about humility before God, now we will consider humility as it concerns us in ourselves.

We need an unassuming estimate of ourselves. We need to be happy that others should take that view of us too. So pride and ostentation are the enemies of these two sorts of humility.

The sin of pride is so great that through it angels fell from heaven. It was the first and is the greatest sin that the devil himself has been guilty of. But more important – God hates pride:

The Lord hates everyone who is arrogant; he will never let them escape punishment. (Proverbs 16.5)

God resists the proud, but gives grace to the humble. (James 4.6)

Since God hates nothing but evil, something that God hates so much must be a very great evil.

Pride has its penalties: it leads to other sins and lays us open to punishment. As humility is the root of all virtue, so is its opposite, pride, the root of all vice. For he who is proud, sets himself up as his own God. So he can't submit to rules or laws except the ones he makes himself.

A wicked man does not care about the Lord; in his pride he thinks that God doesn't matter. (Psalm 10.4)

You see it is the evil man's pride that makes him despise God. Once a man is that proud, he's prepared to commit every sin. We could cite a whole lot of sins that flow naturally from pride: for instance insolence (Proverbs 21.24), impertinence (Proverbs 13.10). For someone who thinks highly of himself expects everyone else to agree with him. He's no option but to fight and quarrel when he thinks people are not taking enough notice of him. I could go on for ever listing fruits that grow on this poisonous tree of pride, but one more will be enough.

Supposing God in his goodness begins to lead to repentance a man who is proud. The proud man won't understand what God is doing, he'll think that the goodness that God is showing to him is a reward – that he deserves it. Nor will he imagine that he needs repentance if God should do it the other way; if he is firm with him. If God brings him trouble, that pride will make him grumble against God. Then if God can't correct his pride, other people won't be able to do it! If the man thinks God's correction is unjust, he's hardly likely to take it from others. Nothing you say to him will be of any avail; for if you warn a proud man – however gently and lovingly – he will look upon it as a disgrace. And instead of admitting the fault and changing his ways, he will turn on you as you try to help him. He will tell you that you're interfering and censorious. Your kindness will only be rewarded by hatred. Someone who resists every cure is obviously in a very dangerous condition.

But there's another danger for the proud man, for he has openly made God his enemy and if you take on such a strong opponent, you're asking for trouble.

Pride leads to destruction, and arrogance to downfall. (Proverbs 16.18)

The Lord hates everyone who is arrogant; he will never let them escape punishment. (Proverbs 16.5)

Evidently, the law is unchangeable; it's no good trying to save a proud man. This is very obvious in the story of Nebuchadnezzar (Daniel 4). Nebuchadnezzar was a king, the most powerful in the world, yet he was driven from men to live with animals because of his pride. This is the sort of judgement we can see happening to proud people in the world around us.

But where nothing happens don't let the proud man think he has escaped God's punishment – there's another world to come.

Good looks, strength and intelligence – these are the things that people are usually proud of. And that's very foolish. For one thing it's easy to be mistaken; to think ourselves handsome or clever when we are not. And there's nothing more ridiculous than to be proud of something we haven't got. We can see other people doing this, but we never notice it in ourselves. There's nothing more despicable than a proud fool! Yet everyone who thinks he is clever is in this danger. Our opinion of ourselves is the most unreliable of all.

But supposing we are right and we do have all these things, how should we be proud of them when there are plenty of creatures who do better? How much more beautiful is the whiteness of a lily and the redness of a rose than the complexion of any human face! How many animals there are who are stronger than men and run faster! There are many animals which act more wisely and more practically than we do. They are often proffered as examples in the Bible. So it's illogical for us to think highly of ourselves when such things are common in the natural world.

And then again, the things that we are proud of don't last. A temper destroys the most outstanding intelligence; sickness rots beauty and strength – or if it doesn't, old age will. Therefore being proud is stupid.

Finally, we didn't give these things to ourselves anyway, so we can't reasonably congratulate ourselves upon them. Wealth and honour (which we may be fortunate to have) – it's foolish to be proud of these things too. They may give us a bit of dash and bravado but they don't make any difference to us as we are. You can load an ass with money, or dress him in rich clothes, but you still can't make him a horse! What is more, these are things which are here today and gone tomorrow. Those who are rich and lose their fortunes don't get much pity from anybody. What's more, wealth and honour don't belong to us anyway; we just look after them for God. We should think about what we owe him rather than what we have got: 'It is the Lord's blessing that makes you wealthy' (Proverbs 10.22). So you see the foolishness of this sort of pride?

Spiritual qualities – how stupid to be proud of these! For they all come from God's work in us. To be proud of something that has really been given by God is the most certain way of losing it. You may remember the parable of Matthew 25.28: the talent was taken away from the one who had put it to no use. What's going to happen to us if, far from putting our talents to no use, we have offered them for Satan's use? It doesn't matter how much good we have done. If we are proud, as far as we are concerned, our well doing becomes a liability.

How stupid it is then to be *proud* of God's grace! It's being like children when they pull to bits the things they are most fond of – it's worse than that, because we don't only lose the thing that we've been given, but also we open ourselves to punishment for pride.

Hate pride; keep watch over your own heart so it never takes root. Don't let it begin to feed on self-esteem. If any such thought arises, beat it down straight away by remembering some occasion when you have been foolish or wrong. Make the slightest movement towards pride an opportunity for humility.

Here's another tip: do you remember the Pharisee who prayed,

> I thank you, God, that I am not greedy, dishonest, or an adulterer, like everybody else. I thank you that I am not like that tax collector over there. I fast two days a week, and I give you a tenth of all my income. (Luke 18.11,12)?

Never compare yourself as better than people who are more foolish or more wicked. If you must make comparison, consider the wise and the godly. Then you will find you come so far short that it will pull you off your pedestal. Finally, pray hard that God will take out every bit of pride that is in you and make you 'poor in spirit' (Matthew 5.3) – the kingdom of heaven belongs to people like this.

The other sin that runs counter to humility is ostentation and the acceptance of flattery. Jesus questions how those who 'like to receive praise from one another' (John 5.44) can believe in God. This sin keeps Christ out of the heart and it opens up the possibility of many others. For anyone who depends on the praises of men will be sure to commit whatever great sin comes into fashion rather than run the risk of being thought too narrow.

What is it that we are looking for? Flattery is nothing but air – the breath of men. It brings us no real advantage. I am no wiser or better because someone *tells* me I am intelligent or good. There's no point in living just to obtain compliments. If they are made to our face and it is not true, it's a great disservice. If they're made behind our backs we don't even get the pleasure of hearing them. So why live for flattery? There's no gain in it.

If you seek praise you're not master of yourself; you have to change all that you do in order to get it. Instead of doing what your own conscience tells you, you do what will bring you compliments. So you become a slave of everybody who flatters you. Worse than that, when you fall short and don't get the praise you want, it is mental torture for you. (If you want a biblical instance of this, read about Ahithophel – 2 Samuel 17.23.) The pain which goes with this sin just proves how foolish it is. And there's more hurt to it yet – because if the flattery is about some good or Christian action, you lose any reward you might have gained from it.

> When you give something to a needy person do not made a big show of it, as the hypocrites do in the houses of worship and on the street. They do it so that people will praise them. I assure you, they have already been paid in full. (Matthew 6.2)

What an exchange for the worse! Who would have men's reward rather than God's? It's like the dog in the fable who saw in the water the reflection of the meat he held in his mouth, tried to catch the reflection and dropped the meat. So we let go the eternal rewards of heaven to catch only a few good words from men.

Here are remedies which will check the first stirrings of the desire for flattery: Never let it become the object of your good deeds. Let duty be your only motive for Christian behaviour. Let reason control your everyday life. Set yourself a better standard – that of pleasing God. Check everything by this standard: Will God approve of it? And then there won't be any question as to what others will say about what you do. If at any time you are praised, don't be too pleased, or think any more of yourself. If it is for some virtue you are praised, remember God was working in you; give him the glory. If it was some chance thing, remember it doesn't deserve praise, because there was no achievement in it. If it was something wrong it ought to set you trembling rather than rejoicing.

> How terrible when all people speak well of you; Their ancestors said the very same thing about the false prophets. (Luke 6.26)

Finally, pray for help to fight the disease of looking for praise.

GENTLENESS

This is a calmness and quietness of spirit quite opposed to impatience and loss of temper. We owe this attitude to God – as we have seen under the heading of humility. But also we owe it to ourselves and reap a great benefit from it. Christ says that such people are blessed by God (Matthew 5.5). And that's not just an other-wordly blessing, but one for this life too! He says, 'They shall inherit the earth' (Matthew 5.5).

In fact nobody apart from the gentle, submissive person has true enjoyment of anything in this world, for irritable and impatient people are ill. They can't even enjoy the best things that come to them. However good the weather outside, they have storms within. Anyone who has seen these wrecks of temper must agree how pleasant a thing is gentle submissiveness.

In this way too we become like Christ:

Take my yoke and put it on you, and learn from me, because I am gentle and humble in spirit; and you will find rest. (Matthew 11.29)

And in this way we conquer ourselves – the greatest and most noble of all victories.

Finally, it is gentleness which gives us dignity as human beings. Anger makes us like animals; fierce and savage. Everybody avoids a man in a temper as they would a ferocious animal. Gentleness is level-headedness and restraint; anger is pure madness. Fury sends a man out of control and causes him to do things that in his right mind he would never do. How many people have done things in anger which they have regretted for the rest of their life?

Here's another advantage of this gentle submissiveness: it makes any situation endurable. It takes the cutting edge from suffering and hardship; anger and bitterness only make misfortune hurt more than it would have done. In some cases they make harmless things into an injury; for instance, what other people say. Words can't hurt us in themselves but they can make us angry; and it is our anger which hurts. Those who ignore harsh words are not adversely affected by them; indeed they are rewarded by God for their patience.

But it is far easier to persuade people to see this than it is to help them put it into practice. Surely there's no-one with such an uncontrollable temper that he can't do something to cure it? Here's how it should be done. Let's start by imprinting deep in our minds the attractiveness and blessings of a gentle spirit. We could contrast it with anger's ugliness and its power for working evil. Then, we must take the example of Christ who endured slander, yes, and torture, with consummate patience; he who was

'lead like a lamb to the slaughter' (Isaiah 53.7); who...
'when he was insulted, did not answer back with an insult; when he suffered, did not threaten'. (1 Peter 2.23)

And if the Lord of glory submitted to such unjust treatment from his own subjects, how can we ever complain of any injury done to us? Watch very carefully for the first beginnings of anger, eliminate all peevishness and petulance. These are sins in themselves. Even if they don't get any further, let them remain unchecked and they will break out into open anger. So if you discover the least beginning of these things, be as quick about dealing with them as you would be if a fire started in your house. And don't add fuel to it by turning it over in your mind. At such a time, watch your tongue; for your breath will fan the flame not only in your opponent but in you as well. The greater the temptation, the more you need to come to God to ask him to help you overcome it. Finally, remember how deserving of God's punishment you have been. Then – whether your troubles come from God or man – you will realise that you are getting far short of what is owing to you, and you will be ashamed that you ever got angry.

SELF-EXAMINATION

The third virtue is reflection upon the state of our souls and our manner of life; what we are doing. We must examine our lives, but not by the easy questions that we draw up to suit ourselves: Do we believe that Christ died for our sins? Do we believe that God has accepted us amongst his chosen people?...etc! If this sort of thing was all that was required to put us in favour with God, no one but the depressed person could ever be otherwise! But in the last resort it's what God says to us in the Bible that matters, so we had better pay heed to that now. Think, whoever continues in any one wilful sin is not in God's favour – nor can he hope for mercy.

Remember the bridesmaids who had to be ready with oil in their lamps when the bridegroom came (Matthew 25). We want to be ready too, because there is only a breath between life and death. So we have to take stock of ourselves.

Then we must watch what we do, thinking first, and not rushing in madly. Before we act we should check our consciences. Anyone who does just what he feels like doing is bound to fall into sin. So think carefully, be sure that a thing is right before you do it. Forethought is advisable anyway, it's part of worldly wisdom. An impulsive person is only one stage better than a fool. With our souls, we need to be even more alert, for they are of great value and in great danger.

As we look back on our actions, we can check them by what Jesus told us to do. We should do this whether we have been good or bad; if good, it will encourage us to do well again – and to thank God for his grace which enables us to do well. If bad, it's even more important that we take stock of our actions. Unless we analyse what we've done it will be impossible to put things right. Without reflection we won't know where we need to improve, and we'll go from one mistake to another.

The more often we examine ourselves, the less likely it is that any of our sins will escape our attention. I recommend that, every night, you run through all the things you have done during the day. If you have done anything wrong, you'll discover it and steel yourself against it in the future, so it won't grow into a habit. What is more, if you do find something, you can ask God to forgive you at the earliest opportunity. It's so much easier to reflect on our lives' short episodes a little at a time while the occasions are fresh in our memory. We really need to say 'sorry' separately for every deliberate sin. We ought to be afraid to sleep without receiving the assurance of God's forgiveness.

CONTENTEDNESS

Contentedness is being satisfied with the circumstances in which God has put us. We don't grumble, but happily welcome whatever God sends. Contentedness is such a delightful virtue because it is the cure for other spiritual sicknesses. When it grows in the heart it subdues not just one, but a whole cluster of other sins.

First of all it gets rid of grumbling – a sin that God hates. As we can see by his punishment of the people of Israel in the desert; you can read the story in the Bible books Exodus and Numbers. It's also a gain to ourselves. How happy is a contented person!

Contentedness quietens ambition. The ambitious man is always dissatisfied with his present situation. That makes him greedily seek a better one. Selfish ambition is not only a sin in itself, but it starts people off on other sins. People who so badly want to be great don't stop at lying, slander, murder – anything that will advance their ambition. And they have considerable pangs of conscience. They are bound to when you think of the fears and jealousies, the worries and anxieties that go along with ambition – let alone the great public ruin that happens in the end. So in this case too, being content is a great happiness as well as a great virtue:

Keep your lives free from the love of money, and be satisfied with what you have. (Hebrews 13.5)

To be content? Or to be money-minded? These are opposites. We can see this from common experience. For the covetous man never thinks he has enough, so he can't be content. Anyone who so longs after something he hasn't got, can never be content. Christ himself tells us, 'You cannot serve both God and money'. (Luke 16.13)

If your heart is besotted with getting rich, it can't be filled with God. And if you watch a money-minded man, he is so busy trying to get wealthy that he has no time or inclination to do his duty by God. If a good bargain comes his way, or the chance to make a profit, prayer and all his religious duties go out of the window. The trouble is that he loves money so much that even if he has to sin against God to get rich, he'll do it.

Those who are mad to get rich don't care about their souls; they sell them to eternal destruction for a little cash.

Surely you know that the wicked will not possess God's kingdom. Do not fool yourselves; people who are immoral...or who steal, or are greedy...or are thieves – none of these will possess God's kingdom. (1 Corinthians 6.9,10)

Covetousness goes right against the duty that we owe to our neighbours. People who have an excessive love of money do not care whom they cheat or defraud in order to gain for themselves. And there's not a chance that a money-minded man will be charitable; he's more worried about his bank balance than his starving brother. We begin to understand what St Paul means when he says,

The love of money is a source of all kinds of evil. Some have been so eager to have it that they have wandered away from the faith and have broken their hearts with many sorrows! (1 Timothy 6.10)

And covetousness is a sin just as miserable as it is evil, for between the anxiety of gaining and the fear of losing, there's no peace. So if you value your happiness – in this world or the next – guard yourself against this sin. And there's no way of doing that except by filling your heart with the virtue of contentedness.

Envy is another vice which is displaced by contentedness. For if you are content with the situation in which you find yourself, you are not tempted to envy anybody else. Envy is a great irritant, it worries and bothers the mind. So what a blessing is the contentedness which frees us from it.

So how shall you come by contentedness? Begin by regarding your state of life as given to you by God. He knows what is best for you and he is much more able to judge than you are. If you are not content with what you have, than you are in effect saying that you know better than God.

Then think how shallow and temporary worldly things are. There's not much to them when we have got them, and we're never sure of keeping them. They won't do anything for us when we die, or when we face God's judgement. If you think of it this way, you won't set your heart on them nor be unsatisfied without them.

The next step: don't fasten your mind on things you haven't got. Many people become dissatisfied with what they have simply by thinking of what they would like to have. It's easy to think when you are looking at somebody else that you would be so happy if you were in his position. But in this way you lose the enjoyment of all you have yourself. And yours could be in many ways a happier life than that of the neighbour which you so much admire. For we look on the outside of other people's lives; and many people whom we think are lucky, in fact have some hidden problem which makes them think quite the opposite. So don't compare yourself with people you think are more prosperous; rather take note of those who are less happy and you will find reason to be glad of your own station in life.

If you consider how little you deserve anything from God, then instead of grumbling you will discover – and be amazed at – God's generosity.

I am not worth all the kindness and faithfulness that you have shown me, your servant. (Genesis 32.10)

Think often of what joy there is for you in heaven, think of heaven as your real home and your life in this world as a journey. The traveller doesn't expect the same comfort on his journey as he does when he arrives home. So be content with whatever you come across, knowing you are travelling to a place of complete happiness which will make up for all the inconvenience and trouble you meet on the way.

Lastly, ask God, who gives everything good, to add to all his blessings that of a contented mind. Without this last gift you won't be able to appreciate the others.

VIGILANCE

Sin, as the greatest danger to our souls, must be the chief object of our vigilance. When a town is besieged, the strongest guard is kept on the weakest part of the wall. It should be the same with you: wherever you find the greatest temptation, there keep special watch. What, then, are you weakest points? Your temperament? The company you keep? Your way of life? To which attacks do they leave you open?

INDUSTRY

We owe God hard work.

> I walked through the fields and vineyards of a lazy, stupid man. They were full of thorn bushes and overgrown with weeds. The stone wall around them had fallen down. I looked at this and thought about it, and learned a lesson from it: have a nap and sleep if you want to. Fold your hands and rest awhile, but while you are asleep, poverty will attack you like an armed robber. (Proverbs 24.30-34)

For God has committed to us the care of our soul as well as our property. Our responsibility towards each is the enhancing of its wealth. And soul has natural and divine wealth. By natural wealth I mean reason, intelligence, memory and so on; by divine wealth I mean the gifts of God – those which do not come naturally but are directly given by him. We must take care to improve both types of wealth for they are talents given to us for this very reason.

The best way of improving our natural gifts is by using them to God's glory. We must not let them become lazy through lack of use, nor should we spoil them by misuse, expending them on base pleasures. Too many people do this. But we must set them to work and put them to good use – make sure it's not in the devil's service. Sadly, many use their intelligence to affront God, cheating their neighbours, stuffing their minds full of dirt that should never have entered their thoughts. As we use our talents, we have to think about God's glory; what we can do to bring glory to God, help our neighbours, and to put our accounts right for the time when God comes to audit them?

> God has given us the very great and precious gifts he promised, so that by means of these gifts you may escape from the destructive lust that is in the world, and may come to share the divine nature. For this very reason do your best to add goodness to your faith; to your goodness add knowledge; to your knowledge add self-control; to your self-control add endurance; to your endurance add godliness; to your godliness add brotherly affection; and to your brotherly affection add love! (2 Peter 1.4-7)

We improve these gifts of God's grace by using them; that is, by doing the things for which the gifts were given. For one thing, when we do something often it becomes easier. For another, we must remember the promise of God.

To every person who has something, even more will be given, and he will have more than enough. But the person who has nothing, even the little that he has will be taken away from him. (Matthew 25.29)

If you put to good use the first gifts of God, more will come. And if you use his further gifts responsibly, there will be even greater yet.

Whenever you find the desire to do good in your heart, think, 'This is the chance to exercise my spiritual responsibility.' If you have even a twinge of conscience against some sin you're harbouring, turn it into a hatred of that sin. And the hatred into a resolve; and when you have made your resolve, do something about it. If you follow this advice persistently and honestly, you will find God helping you all along the way until you can claim a victory over the sin. As you work at it, pray too for God's promises,

Your Father in heaven will give good things to those who ask him. (Matthew 7.11)

If you don't ask you have no right to an answer. Pray sincerely – reflecting the importance of the matter in hand. For fighting sin is more important than anything else in the world, so we must pray with great energy and deep sincerity – more than for any outward gift we ask for.

Supposing you don't exercise and improve the gifts God has given you? What happens then?

From the person who has nothing, even the little that he has will be taken away. (Matthew 25.29)

If we neglect God's gifts, then he takes them away – that's the meaning of the parable. The one who hid his master's money got no profit from it, for his master had it taken away from him. That is the greatest and the worst punishment that can happen to any of us before we come to hell. It's the foretaste of hell, it's being made over to the power of the devil – we are banished from the face of God – and committed to worse misery in another world; for this is what happened to the bad useless servant:

Throw him outside in the darknesss; there he will cry and grind his teeth. (Matthew 25.30)

See how dangerous it is to neglect God's gifts! If we care about our souls at all we must set ourselves to the task of using and improving them.

PURITY

Purity excludes not only adultery, but all forms of sexual adventure outside marriage. And my own opinion is that even within marriage it's best to be restrained; dedicating sexual relations to the purpose of having a family and to strengthening the faithfulness of one to the other. Purity is not only concerned with avoiding gross immorality; we need to be wide awake to every possiblity of sin. We have to control our eyes and hands:

> If your right eye causes you to sin, take it out and throw it away! It is much better for you to lose a part of your body than to have your whole body thrown into hell. If your right hand causes you to sin, cut it off and throw it away! It is much better for you to lose one of your limbs than for your whole body to go to hell. (Matthew 5.29,30)

And we have to watch what we say:

> Do not use harmful words, but only helpful words, the kind that build up and provide what is needed, so that what you say will do good to those who hear you. (Ephesians 4.29)

Yes, and we have to watch even our thoughts and fantasies, we must not entertain any sordid desires. If you refrain from the gross acts of immorality and yet let yourself loose with these private sins, one might be forgiven for suspecting that it is only the social restraint that keeps you from the outward sin. For all are as bad in God's sight. Besides if you let yourself dwell on the possibility of doing immoral things, you are far more likely to do them. So remember that God sees not only our actions but also our hearts, and he loves purity there.

How replusive is this sort of sin! What animals it makes of us. It befuddles our minds and damages our soul. The writer of Proverbs says of the young man seduced,

> Suddenly he was going with her like an ox on the way to be slaughtered, like a deer prancing into a trap where an arrow would pierce its heart. He was like a bird going into a net – he did not know that his life was in danger. (Proverbs 7.22,23)

The results of immoral indulgence are no better for the body than they are for the mind. How many people have made themselves martyrs for the devil's sake! Anybody who pays for this sort of damnation deserves to enjoy for a while what they have bought!

But God's judgement is more important. Remember what happened to Sodom and Gomorrah (Genesis 19.4-29); to Ammon (2 Samuel 13); to Zimri and Cozbi (Numbers 25.8). And do not forget what God says through St. Paul:

> Surely you know that you are God's temple and that God's Spirit lives in you! So if anyone destroys God's temple, God will destroy him. For God's temple is holy, and you yourselves are his temple. (1 Corinthians 3.16,17)

The sin of immorality shuts us out from the kingdom of heaven, for no impure thing can enter there. Paul after listing the consequences of immoral human nature says,

> I warn you now as I have before; those who do these things will not possess the Kingdom of God. (Galatians 5.19-21)

And again, to the Corinthians:

> Surely you know that the wicked will not possess God's Kingdom. (1 Corinthians 6.9)

There again he lists the various aspects of immorality and perversion. If we pollute ourselves we are fit company only for evil spirits, for the devil and his angels, where the flames of our lust will boost the furnaces of hell.

I have piled on the agony to recommend to you the virtue of purity. If you want it you will have to be very careful to clamp down on the first beginnings of each temptation. Once you establish a détente and begin talks with temptation, it gains on you still more and you find it harder to resist. In such circumstances the best way is to run rather than fight. Laziness of course is the perfect soil for these unpleasant weeds to grow in, so keep busy in worthwhile things and don't think back over disreputable acts that you have taken part in. For that is reliving the sin again as far as God is concerned. Pray to God for the Spirit of purity, especially when temptation is close; bring the particular 'devil' to Christ to be cast out. And if it won't be cast out by prayer alone, add fasting.

MODERATION

Moderation applies to eating, drinking, sleeping, recreation, and what we buy to wear.

God in his mercy has given us food – for our bodies' very existence and for their well being. Now, for that purpose, moderate eating is appropriate. But if we eat to pamper ourselves, and in the service of our excessive appetite, we thwart God's purposes. Then eating itself becomes detrimental to our health.

So we must be careful what we eat and how much we eat – it will differ from person to person. A simple and balanced diet is obviously the most beneficial.

How ridiculous it is to subject the whole body to misuse by enslaving it to this one sense of taste! And yet the indulgent person will sacrifice his soul to his appetite. Think how short-lived is the pleasure – gone in a moment! But the discomfort lasts. A Christian who has a clear sight of the joys of the spiritual world can see these gross pleasures for what they are. Remember what happened to the indulgent man who

> dressed in the most expensive clothes and lived in great luxury every day ... He called out in Hades, 'Father Abraham! Take pity on me, and send Lazarus to dip his finger in some water and cool my tongue beacuse I am in great pain in this fire!' (Luke 16.19,24)

And take note of what Jesus says:

> Be on your guard! Don't let yourselves become occupied with too much feasting and drinking and with the worries of this life. (Luke 21.34)

SOBRIETY

We drink to live and to keep healthy. And whatever we drink should serve this purpose. So that much the same rules apply to drinking as to eating. But there's need for special care with drinking because drink can affect our minds as well as promote our health. In order to be healthy, we mustn't sin, and drunkenness is sin. It's quite evident from the number of drunkards there are in the world that many drink for reasons other than their health!

The most accepted reason is for company's sake. One man drinks to keep the other company. But I question the logic of this – if it were poison that the first man were drinking, would the second man join him for company's sake? Immoderate drinking is rather like poison – it doesn't kill you on the spot, but it could well bring death in the end.

However, it's the damage which drink does now – not in the future – that should deter a wise man from excessive alcohol. Drink brings on stupidity and bad temper; it turns man into an animal by drowning the rationality which should differentiate him from animals. If drink had been invented by a statesman for punishment, we would have branded him a tyrant!

Then there is social drinking – to keep up friendship and express kindness to each other. It's an extraordinary logic to be kind in a way that brings damage to the other person. Do you befriend a man by destroying his character, his property and his life? It's an odd way of keeping friendship – it must have been a drunk who thought up that one! Besides, experience proves that drink is more likely to lead to quarrelling than to friendship.

Then there is drinking to cheer yourself up. Well, if you have to throw reason out of the window to be happy, it's not worth it! And drunken happiness is short-lived because things people do under the influence of drink only bring misery.

Then they say drink drowns your sorrows. What are these sorrows? Ought they to be drowned? Is it remorse that has to be charmed away? It probably works very well – quieting your conscience by drink. But it's a sinner's stupidity. Are these promptings of conscience justified? If they are to be ignored, why do they bother you? It's impossible to silence them forever. The longer you shut them up the louder they will yell at you. Take a thief or a murderer, frightened of being caught. Do you think he would get drunk to drown the fear of being caught and punished? Of course not; if he had any sense he would keep sober and make good his escape. Yet you are in the same position if your conscience is speaking to you and you silence it with drink. Eventually you must be judged by God, so isn't it better to think about the danger now, and ask him to forgive you?

It may of course be straightforward anxiety that you want to banish from your life. There's a Christian way of doing that; a better way than by drinking:

Leave all your worries with God, because he cares for you. (1 Peter 5.7)

Besides, if you get drunk you are only adding trouble, because when you become sober again your anxieties will return with greater force and bring a new problem with them – the guilt which comes from being drunk.

How about drinking to while away the time? This is quite as unreasonable as the other reasons for drinking. And in addition, it shows up your idleness – a wretched thing in itself. You must be able to find *something* to do. Even if you have little work of your own, there's much that can be done to help other people. If you still have spare time you have a soul to look after! Where there are so many sins which can kill, so many temptations to keep us watchful (drunkenness is not the least of these), so much grace that God can give to strengthen and energise us, so many wrongs to repent of, surely there's never a lack of something to do; all these take up time. Or so dying people find – for those who have worked all their lives to while away the time, would then give all the world to buy it back again. It may be you don't have much leisure, so this point is lost on you. But when you do have time to yourself, remember that it's better spent for the blessing of your soul rather than the ruin of it. And drinking ruins souls.

Then there's drinking to be popular; to avoid being mocked for high principles. But what harm can such mockery do compared with the evil of drunkeness? Besides, Jesus says that to accept such ridicule is the path to being truly happy:

> Happy are you when people insult you and persecute you and tell all kinds of evil lies against you because you are my followers. (Matthew 5.11)

> Happy are you if you are insulted because you are Christ's followers; this means that the glorious Spirit, the Spirit of God, is resting on you. (1 Peter 4.14)

To be laughed at for obeying any commandment Jesus made, is to be laughed at for his sake. We should remember that in the baptism service we promised to fight under the banner of Christ against sin, the world, and the devil, and to continue his faithful soldiers and servants to the end of our lives. Shall we now run away because of a few scornful remarks? What is worse – other people's laughter? Or God's anger and the threat of hell? And if you are sensitive to the scorn of other people why do you do what is bound to bring you scorn in the end: getting drunk? Remember the sentence Christ Jesus passes on those who are ashamed of him:

> If a person is ashamed of me and of my teaching in this godless and wicked day, then the Son of Man will be ashamed of him when he comes in the glory of his Father with the holy angels. (Mark 8.38)

If you want to play about with sin for the sake of other people's opinion of you, then you deserve to be disowned by Christ. When all is said and done, you can't be sure that your friends will despise you for being sober. They may pretend to despise you in order to egg you on but, if the truth were known or if they would admit it, you would find they had a silent respect for people with self-control. In fact those that follow their way bear the brunt of much laughter: the drunk is the butt of many jokes.

Though few will admit it, the other reason for drinking is its pleasure. People who feel like this about drinking are not going to listen to persuasion. What can be said about someone who sells his health, his reason, his God, his soul for drink when he doesn't need to? Take my advice, all those of you who go in for drinking for social reasons, it could only be a matter of time before you get into the drunken ways which you pretend to despise. Those who drink for company's sake often end up addicted – it happens every day.

Last of all, there's drinking for business purposes. They say it is necessary to drink in order to strike up a good bargain with your acquaintance. This is worse than all the rest! You are drinking to cheat and defraud someone – that's the top and bottom of it. We think that when others are slightly the worse for drink we shall be able to persuade them the more easily. Don't forget that it can work the other way round! For those who take someone drinking hoping to get the better of them may prove less resilient and get drunk first. That gives the intended victim the opportunity of doing all the cheating!

I have shown you how illogical are the reasons which people use to indulge in this sin. Let me go further, let me say this: it's not only being dead drunk that's a sin, but the leser degrees of being drunk which affect your mind – either by dulling it and making it less fit for work, or by lightening it and making you frivolous, liable to fall about and crack stupid jokes or worse, working the drinker up into a flaming temper. These effects or anything else that makes a change in the personality are to be counted in the sin of drunkenness. Indeed, drinking beyond moderate refreshment – which is its proper purpose – is a sin, even if it doesn't make the least change in a man. In other words, anyone who doesn't easily get drunk but can spend whole days – or a good part of them anyway – in drinking, is far from being innocent. For even though such drinking doesn't seem to affect his intelligence, yet his life's purpose is the same as the drunkard – to pour down drink. So he's liable to the same judgement.

> You are doomed; heroes of the wine bottle; brave and fearless when it come to mixing drinks! (Isaiah 5.22)

The drunkard is guilty of waste. First: God's gift of drink is intended for refreshment and relief of thirst; it's abused and misspent when drunk so far beyond our needs. Second: It's a waste of time given to us by God in which to 'work out our salvation'. (Philippians 2.12) Our time must be strictly accounted for, therefore every minute must be carefully ordered for the purpose of wise living.

If you drink excessively, although you might escape being drunk yourself, yet you are guilty of any drunkenness your friends might fall into. For you have given them encouragement to drink by your example – especially if you are someone who is respected. If you are popular with your friends, you are guilty of leading them into a trap, for they would sooner drink with you than lose your friendship. What's worse is the deliberate attempt by those who can hold their drink to get their fellows drunk. They count it an achievement to make others fall, as though there was some prize for it. By this we make ourselves the devil's workmen, trying our hardest to bring our brothers into eternal unhappiness. This is the top rung of the vice of drinking – adding to our own excesses the sin of hurting others. The world might think it funny, but God threatens:

> Woe to him who gives drink to his neighbours, pouring it from the wine-skin till they are drunk, so that he can gaze on their naked bodies. You will be filled with shame instead of glory. Now it is your turn! Drink and be exposed! The cup from the Lord's right hand is coming round to you, and disgrace will cover your glory. (Habakkuk 2.15,16)

Such a pastime, you see, can be very expensive indeed.

I have gone into this sin in detail because it has got such a stranglehold on us. It affects all walks of life, all ages and both sexes. It ruins not only our souls for the life to come, but our chances and our happiness now. There's nothing like this sin for bringing other problems with it; damage to your mind, health, standing and property. And there's every reason to believe that drinking has been too common and too long with us nationally, and has brought down many of the troubles that have afflicted us.

So, Christian reader, let me plead with you – no, severely warn you – not to get involved. These are the reasons:

1. Your love for God and his honour.

2. The reputation of the Christian faith.

3. The well being of your own eternal soul.

4. The good of the Church and the nation of which you are a member.

    5. Your own health and position in the world.

Think about all these things and then see if there is sufficient
pleasure to be had from drunkenness to make up for all the troubles
it brings with it. I'm sure that anybody with any intelligence
wouldn't think so.

If you do drink too much, then be ashamed of your foolishness,
of making a bad bargain. Start now: decide never again to be guilty
of this stupid sin. However often you have fallen into it in the past,
fear God now, and abstain. If you do that, you will find that you've
made a good change; anybody who has tried both ways of life will
admit from his heart that there's infinitely more satisfaction to be
had in being sober and moderate than ever there was from
drinking-bouts.

The chief problem is breaking the habit, for we have brought an
artificial thirst on ourselves, and our bodies seem to need the drink.
Patience is required, and time – though even a few days will make
all the difference. If you think it's hard to break, think of the
consequences of failure, as though it were some disease that would
eventually kill you. Resolve to put up with the pain for a little while
and you will have conquered your problem.

Then comes the question: how do you fill up the time which you
used to spend drinking? No sooner asked than answered: find some
work to get involved in. That shouldn't be difficult for those who
have to work for their living.

A further difficulty comes from the company of other people.
Your former companions are going to make fun of you, and try to
get you back to the drink. They will tell you how unkind it is to
reject their company; that it is impolite not to 'have one' with
them; that it's a shame not to be merry and hearty. If that doesn't
work they'll try and tease you out of it.

To be forewarned is to be forearmed. When you first get started
on abstinence you need to reckon that these and other temptations
will come. Weigh it up beforehand. Think whether the 'good time'
you have drinking socially is worthy to be compared with the real
and eternal fellowship of God which is lost by it; whether the false
happiness of drinking rates higher than the pleasure of a clear
conscience or the joy of heaven to come. Is the mocking of other
people – the reproach of the world and wicked men – as bad as the
accusations of your own conscience now, and the shame of eternal
judgement then? Weigh it all up, I tell you.

Not only from the religious point of view, but from the angle of
common sense we are forced to agree that the gains of moderation

completely outweigh the arguments against. When you come to this conclusion you have to resolve accordingly, and when any of these testings of your resolve come along you can reflect that you've thought it all out; you know how much weight they should carry with you and that for the sake of what you lose they're not worth taking any notice of. Hold tight to what you've decided and angrily reject all suggestions to the contrary.

Be sure that you resist from the very beginnning, and don't give in at all, for as soon as you give ground you are lost. This is a creeping sin and it will get a hold on you. Sadly we see many who have decided to give up drinking get careless and venture into bad company. They are persuaded, to take one drink...and then another and another, until in the end they are drinking as freely as the rest. And all the resolutions they made when they were sober are drowned.

So, whoever you are, if you really mean to give up this sin, make sure you have no opportunity to start again. It's worth telling everybody your intention, to stop them trying to persuade you to drink. But if you are timid about abstaining, they'll soon make use of your weakness and break your resolve.

Watch for the beginnings of this sin and you'll never be overtaken by it. It's like our nation's defence – there's no danger as long as we are constantly on the alert, but either surprise, or deterioration renders us open to attack. Watch for subtle erosion of your defences:

He who despises small beginnings will fall little by little. (Ecclesiasticus 19.1)

Then pray sincerely to God that he too will watch out for you and with his strength help you to resist all temptations to this sin. If you are absolutely sincere about it you'll defeat this vice however long you've been drinking.

Perhaps because everybody does it and you enjoy it, or because you've become so used to it and love it, you feel your drink habit can't be very wrong. You think it won't hurt you and you tend to reassure yourself and hope that either it isn't a sin or that it is only a little one that won't keep you out of heaven. Don't deceive yourself. You might as well say there is no heaven, as that drunkenness won't keep you out:

Do not fool yourselves; people who are immoral or who worship idols or are adulterers...or are drunkards...none of these will possess God's kingdom. (1 Corinthians 6.9,10)

And even if it's not obvious from texts like this, commonsense will tell us that heaven is a place of infinite purity, and we can't live there until our bodies are changed – refined and purified – as St. Paul tells us (1 Corinthians 15.53). We're going to be worse not better if we've changed ourselves into pigs! We're more ready for devils to enter into us, as they did to the herd at Gadara (Mark 5.13). And don't we see cases of this every day? For where drunkenness takes hold of a person it is usually the first of many problems. Every drunken bout gets a man ready for another sin; lust, temper and all the animal appetites are let loose.

If what I have said is not enough to scare you out of your drinking, you might as well choke on it and stay senseless until hell's flames wake you up! Then you'll find out by sad experience what you won't believe now: 'These things result in death'. (Romans 6.21)

May God in his infinite mercy wake up in time everybody who dabbles in this sin, so that by defeating it they might escape from God's anger that will come eventually.

IN RELAXATION

Sleep was given by God to refresh and sustain our weak bodies. Hard work tires and wearies them and sleep comes as medicine for that weariness. Sleep repairs decay; sleep gives us new strength for the work which God gives us. Sleep was intended to make us more efficient, not more lazy! You don't rest a horse because you are pleased with it, but so that you may get better service from it.

How do we know the difference between proper rest and laziness? If it refreshes us, and makes us more lively and fit for action, then that's moderate sleep and it's the amount we need. Obviously some people need more than others – that's the way they're made. Everybody has to judge from their own experience. But be honest about it! – remember the 'sluggard':

I walked through the fields and vineyards of a lazy, stupid man. They were full of thorn-bushes and overgrown with weeds. The stone walls around them had fallen down. I looked at this, thought about it, and learned a lesson from it: Have a nap and sleep if you want to. Fold your hands and rest awhile, but while you are asleep, poverty will attack you like an armed robber. (Proverbs 24.30)

If we do not discipline ourselves with regard to sleeping, we fall into various traps set by the sin of laziness. We waste the time which God gives us for using well. We damage our bodies by not

using them – experience shows that we need exercise and movement to avoid disease. We injure our souls too. The lazy body can't
serve the soul in its Christian duty, and both become useless and
unfit for the work for which God has designed them. Worst of all we
ignore God's wishes because he made us to obey him and serve him
actively. If we sleep away our lives, we do the very opposite.

But laziness is not just a matter of sin, it's also damaging in other
ways; our state of life will suffer; if we are lazy we will never
succeed.

> If all you do is eat and sleep, you will soon be wearing rags.
> (Proverbs 23.21)

In fact it can hardly be said that the really lazy person lives at all!
Sleep, then, is a kind of death and if you sacrifice yourself to it you
will only die before your time.

IN OUR ENTERTAINMENT

We have to very careful to avoid any element of sin in our
entertainment. We must not for pleasure's sake do anything that
dishonours God or hurts somebody else. That is just what happens
with those who indulge in blasphemy, pornography or spiteful
humour. No, we should be moderate with our entertainment: not
spending too much time on it; remembering that its purpose is to
refresh us for our work, and that it's not an end in itself. And we
musn't get so enthusiastic about our pleasures that they consume
us, for then they take our minds off the lasting things of life. Then
we are just like children who after their school break can't get down
to work again.

We must never use entertainment just to pass our time. We
ought to be studying how to use time profitably (Ephesians 5.15-17
– 'making our calling and election sure'), not just flinging it away.
How can those who spend whole days and nights gambling justify
it? Time wasn't given for this! What sort of account of themselves
are they going to give? Time is a precious treasure and they throw
it away!

We must try to keep covetousness out of our entertainment. If
we are going to play a game of sport let it be for recreation, not to
win money. Keep the profit motive out of your entertainment. If
you let it get in you're open to two dangers: one, covetousness –
bringing greed into your sport; the other, loss of temper if you lose.
These things will in turn involve other sins. Covetousness will

tempt you to cheat. Losing your temper will bring swearing and cursing – we see it so often. If you find that you tend to fall into either of these traps in your recreation then you must either take some action to prevent it happening, or you must withdraw from your game altogether . Not that your misuse makes the game wrong, but it becomes wrong for you if sin creeps in.

Christ has told us to avoid temptations with such vigour that if our eyes or our hands offend us we are better parted from them than drawn into sin by them. So much for games by which we risk offending God. If you play, you gamble with your soul and that's too big a price to offer. Besides, you lose the recreation and sport which were the purpose of the game; they become secondary, and the game itself becomes hard work. And you're supposed to be relaxing! Being covetous, being angry, with all the attendant pains and bitterness – these things wear you out.

IN OUR DRESS

And the Lord God made clothes out of animal skins for Adam and his wife and he clothed them. (Genesis 3.21)

When you recall that the wearing of clothes was the consequence of sin, they are not something to be too proud of. The thought should make us humble, for the innocence we lost was much more attractive than smart clothes can ever be. Our clothes are to cover our shame.

But clothes are more than this. We wear them to keep warm. We cut clean across this common sense rule when sheer vanity makes us wear clothes which are so thin or uncomfortable that we catch cold or worse. Then, our bodies are hurt rather than helped. It's a stupid way of going on, but very common with those who are clothes-conscious.

God's instruction in the Jewish law is that men and women should be distinguished by wearing dissimilar clothes. But clothes also distinguish states of life. We should be content with the clothing that matches our situation, not trying to be the best-dressed in order to put ourselves a few rungs higher up the ladder. Dress moderately in order to suit your calling in life. Do not resent it if others have better clothes.

Remember that clothes don't add any real value to a person. So it is simply not good enough to spend a major part of your time thinking about or spending a lot of your money on them. You shouldn't value yourself more because of what you are able to afford, or despise others who can't afford to dress well. When you are choosing what you are going to wear, remember St. Peter's advice to the women of his time:

> Your beauty should not come from outward adornment, such as braided hair and the wearing of gold jewellery and fine clothes. Instead it should be that your inner self, the unfading beauty of a gentle and quiet spirit, which is of great worth in God's sight. (1 Peter 3.3,4)

Dress yourself with real Christian goodness – that's the clothing which will make you attractive in God's eyes – and to the eyes of other people too. For unless your onlookers are idiots they will value you more for being good than for being ostentatious. And one ordinary coat you give to a poor friend will make you look much better than twenty plush coats you put on your own back.

Although I've talked of moderation in detail, I want to add this warning. I have been highlighting the fault of *excess*, yet it's quite possible to fall into the opposite error – of being so miserly or careless of health and limb that you don't look after yourselves properly. There are those who are so busy in their jobs that they deprive themselves of the adequate sleep and the recreation that they really need. In other words, don't read what I have said so far and pat yourself on the back because of your self-restraint, when you are so busy getting money that you haven't got time to eat!

> The love of money is a source of all kinds of evil. Some have been so eager to have it that they have wandered away from the faith and have broken their hearts with many sorrows. (1 Timothy 6.10)

3

Our Duty to Others

Included in St. Paul's 'righteousness' is not only *living correctly*, but every kind of *charity* too. For by the law of Christ we owe love to our neighbour, and it is 'unrighteousness' when we deprive him of it. So I am going to talk about duty to our neighbour under the general headings of Justice and Love.

JUSTICE

There's passive and active justice. The first requires that we do no wrong or injury to anyone; we may not hurt either his soul or his body, his possessions or his reputation. So this passive justice requires restraint from us.

What harm could we do to our neighbour's soul? We can't touch it, so surely no weapon can hurt it? True, yet it is capable of being hurt or wounded – even to death. The soul can be wounded with grief or sadness: 'Heart-ache crushes the spirit'. (Proverbs 15.13)

So we must not needlessly hurt or grieve our neighbour. This is the way of malicious and spiteful people; they will do things simply to hurt others. What a savage and inhuman attitude to take pleasure in other people's unhappiness! Whoever enjoys it might well be considered to have a devil in him, for demons delight in misery.

We must remember that the soul can be hurt in a deeper sense, for souls are spiritual and immortal. So that whoever incites other people to sin, betrays their souls to God's punishment. And who-ever gives another a mortal wound is guilty of his death. Surely there can't be anthing worse we could do than to bring great evil upon someone's soul?

There are a number of ways in which we can so wound somebody else. If you have authority over somebody, and you make him do something which is wrong, that is one way. In the Bible we might instance Nebuchadnezzar commanding his people to worship the golden image (Daniel 3.4). Any parent acts like Nebuchadnezzar if a child is made to do something wrong. Any manager is like Nebuchadnezzar if he makes an employee do something wrong. What's more, we can hurt someone simply by advising, encouraging, or persuading them to do evil. We can induce people to sin by telling them that it is pleasurable or profitable. That too is helping someone to do wrong.

EXAMPLE

If we set the wrong example, we're not directly responsible for somebody else's sin; nevertheless we have done our part in their downfall. Usually people don't need much more than a bad example to do wrong. And you can encourage them in their sin either by overtly approving, or at least by not showing your dislike for it.

We might also defend, or try to justify something somebody else has done wrong. In this way we not only sanction what they do but also open the way for others to do the same – others who may be more inclined to do it when they hear it excused by us. Finally, we can be critical about Christian behaviour, or else make fun of it – as many do who tilt at religion. This puts people off doing their duty. For they see they are going to be laughed at. It can make people give up their Christian behaviour altogether.

It would take me too long to list all the different sins which we can draw others into – there's drunkenness, immorality, rebellion against authority – many more. But it's worth your thinking very carefully what trouble you may have brought to someone else by all or any of these means. People all too easily say that they never harm anyone else, but God knows how many who boast like this are really most hurtful. They may not have coshed and robbed their neighbour, but that's only the physical side of it – it's the soul of the man that they can hurt, and bring eternal ruin upon him. For if you have enticed anyone to sin, you've done your part to make hell certain for him. So think how treacherous this is, if you pretend tc be a friend and secretly stab him. The soul is of far more value than the body, and hell worse than death.

In all this you musn't forget how dangerous to yourself it is to lead somebody else into sin. Jesus told us,

> Things that make people fall into sin are bound to happen, but how terrible for the one who makes them happen! It would be better for him if a large mill-stone were tied round his neck and

he were thrown into the sea than for him to cause one of these little ones to sin. So watch out what you do! (Luke 17.1-3)

You may plunge your poor brother over the cliff into hell but, as often happens with those who struggle, both can fall and you'll go down with him; you'll keep him company in that place of torture.

So let the danger that you and he are in warn you away from such injustice to your neighbour. Think how cruel you have been to those whom you have encouraged to get drunk, advised to rebel, caused to lust, inflamed with temper; those whom you have discouraged and disheartened by your cynical approach to faith. Then you had better draw up a list of charges and prosecute yourself as a murderer of your brother. Be very sorry for every wrong of this kind and determine never to do it again:

> You should decide never to do anything that would make your brother stumble or fall into sin. (Romans 14.13)

Your repentance must bear fruit. How can you make up for this damage to your brother's soul? You have robbed him of his innocence, of his title to heaven. You must try to restore these things by being even much more energetic and sincere in winning his repentance than you were in leading him to do wrong. Use as much skill to convince him of his danger as ever you did to persuade him of the pleasures of vice. In other words use all those methods to save him that you did to destroy him.

RESTRAINT

We may wrong each other's bodies. And the highest degree of wrong is murder. God's law forbid this in the sixth commandment: 'Do not commit murder' (Exodus 20.13; Deuteronomy 5.17).

Murder may be the result of direct violence, or it can be done secretly and treacherously: David murdered Uriah, not with his own sword but by putting him in the path of enemy attack (2 Samuel 11.17). Jezebel murdered Naboth by telling lies about him (1 Kings 21.13). Murder can be sudden or coldly calculating. It may originate in an old grievance, come from ambition, or be a cover-up for other misdemeanours.

Suppose we persuade somebody to do something which shortens his life – isn't that murder too? If I get someone drunk and then he goes out and has an accident which causes his death, then it's my fault. Even if he doesn't die from it, but his drinking brings on alcoholism, which kills him, I can't be totally free from blame.

Heavy responsibility also lies on those who stir up trouble between others; they must have a share of the guilt if someone gets killed; that ought to make us wary of ever starting or of inflaming an argument.

Let's look at the nature of the sin of murder. It is a deep dark sin, a sin which cries aloud for justice. God told Cain that his brother Abel's blood cried out from the ground like a voice calling for revenge (Genesis 4.10). The guilt of this sin is so strong that is leaves a stain on every land where it is committed. In the law of Deuteronomy (19.12,13), the land could not be rid of the effects of a murder except by the execution of the murderer. In other cases of wrong, the felon was safe if he ran to the altar of God, yet no refuge was allowed to a wilful murderer. He had to be taken – even from the altar – and handed over for justice.

> When a man gets angry and deliberately kills another man, he is to be put to death, even if he has run to my altar for safety. (Exodus 21.14)

> Man was made like God, so whoever murders a man will himself be killed by his fellow-man. (Genensis 9.6)

The reason for the strictness of this law is in these words:

> Then God said, 'And now we will make human beings; they will be like and resemble us.' (Genesis 1.26)

The sin of murder is not only any injury to someone else, but also is the highest contempt for God himself – it's defacing his image which he has stamped upon humanity. Further, it's usurping God's proper authority: for it is God alone who has the right to give and take away life. Whoever murders somebody takes, as it were, this power from God's hand – the highest degree of rebellious presumption.

The punishment for murder comes in proportion to the gravity of the sin. We see how terrible the penalty is in this world, let alone the fearful effects in the next. Blood cries for vengeance and the great God of recompense will not fail to hear those cries. There are many examples in the Bible of those who killed and as a result perished miserably themselves. History similarly illustrates the consequences of murder.

It is worth noticing how God uses unusual and almost miraculous means to uncover this sin. Even animals – a dog, a cat, a horse – can betray a murderer. The murderer's own horror at this crime sometimes makes him betray himself. So a man cannot use secrecy to defend himself from punishment. In spite of him his conscience knows all, and very often shouts it to the world. Even if it doesn't do that, it has its own revenge on him: to live with his conscience is sheer hell inside him, and worse than death. Many who have committed murder have never enjoyed another minute's peace. Such has been the unbearable pain of their conscience that they have taken their own life rather than go on living with it. If these are the effects on the murderer in this world, then those of the world to come are even more dreadful.

Just thinking about this ought to horrify us at the awesomeness of this sin and make us extremely wary not fall into it ourselves. We'll want to avoid every occasion which might subconsciously lead us into this pit. If you don't want to kill somebody in temper, make sure you are never in a temper. If you permit yourself bad temper you can have no certainty that you won't commit murder, because temper prevents us from thinking what we're doing once it's got hold of us. So when you find yourself beginning to get worked up think where it's going to lead you and smother it quickly. To make sure that hatred won't lead you to murder, be sure not to harbour any hurtful intention in your heart. Once it settles there it will get so strong that in a short while you'll be under its power. Then it can lead you to this horrible sin at its pleasure. It's the same with envy, ambition, lust, or any other wrong desire: don't let them get to grips with you, for once they get the upper hand, as they do, they will be past your control. Then they will rush you into this or any other sin which serves their purpose.

Again, if you don't want to be guilty of any of the fatal effects of somebody else's drinking, make sure you don't invite him to drink, or keep company with him in it. For a start, don't get into the habit yourself. If you do, you will be trying to involve others all the time.

Finally, don't start or encourage hatred or argument – which might lead to murder in the long run. For when you have started a fire, who knows which way it's going to burn?

Although murder might be the greatest crime, it is not the only injury that can be done to our neighbour. The next in degree is maiming him.

We need no other way of measuring the seriousness of this crime than our own attitude to the loss of a limb. We think no danger too great to keep our arms and legs. How wrong we are, then, if we make others suffer in this way! And it's worse if they use their arms or their legs for their work – to buy their food.

> Bread is life to the destitute, and it is murder to deprive them of it. To rob your neighbour of his livelihood is to kill him, and the man who cheats his worker of his wages sheds blood. (Ecclesiasticus 34.21,22)

So if you deprive a man of his income, by disabling him, you yourself are guilty.

In the Old Testament law, it was permitted to everyone who had sustained such damage from his neighbour to ask the magistrate to inflict similar injury:

> Wherever hurt is done, you shall give life for life, eye for eye, tooth for tooth, hand for hand, foot for foot, burn for burn, bruise for bruise, wound for wound. (Exodus 21.23-25)

Revenge is not allowed to us as Christians, yet surely it is the responsibility of everyone who has done such injury to make whatever satisfaction lies in his power. You can't restore a limb (which should make you very careful not to do things which you can't put right). But at least you can try to lessen some of the ill effects of the loss you have inflicted. If you have brought the man to poverty, you must relieve and support him even if it means extra work for you. If as Job suggests (Job 29.15) it is the duty of us all to be 'eyes to the blind and feet to the lame', how much more should we be eyes to those whom we ourselves have made blind, or feet to those we have made lame? So if any of you have injured another, know that you are bound to do all that is possible to set it right. If you don't, every new suffering because of you becomes a new charge against you in the supreme court of God the Judge.

Another degree of injury is wounding. Wounding somebody else may not cause loss of life or limb, but it endangers both. In any case, wounding brings pain, and pain of all ills is the greatest because it is not only an ill in itself, but it won't let us enjoy anything good in life. If you think wounding is a terribly great crime, think how you'd like it if you were in such pain that you couldn't enjoy anything.

The truth is that such twisted cruelty to other people comes from pride and arrogance on our part; we hold others in such contempt that we don't think it matters what we do to them. We think it's acceptable if we hurt other people, while we are so tender to ourselves that we can't hear the least word of criticism without getting ruffled! If we weren't so proud and bad-tempered that every little thing set us on edge we would never be tempted to get violent.

Some people can be so cruel that they don't need provocation. They can hurt their brothers and sisters in cold blood – to entertain their own degraded taste. The Romans made it one of their public sports to see men kill each other. If we take delight in such sights we are as far from being Christian as they were.

This sort of cruelty is so inhuman that men are not even allowed to use it to animals; it's quite intolerable then to set against each other human beings who have the same eternal hopes as we do.

It's no excuse for people to say that what they did was only in return for some injury received from the other person, for even if you have been severely wronged, you can't be your own avenger. Just because someone is your enemy, he's not your servant or slave to do what you like with. You have no power of authority over his body simply because he's wronged you. So if you do retaliate, you are not only unloving – which is a sin in itself – but unjust in any act of violence you may commit against him. Such justice goes higher; it encroaches on God's rights and prerogatives. St Paul warns us,

> Never take revenge, my friends, but instead let God's anger do it. For the Scripture says, 'I will take revenge, I will pay back, says the Lord'. (Romans 12.19)

If you offend against this rule you have, as it were, taken the right of justice out of God's hands and expressed contempt for his divine majesty.

OTHERS' FAMILIES

> Do not desire another man's house; do not desire his wife, his slaves, his cattle, his donkeys, or anything else that he owns. (Exodus 20.17; Deuteronomy 5.21)

A husband's special and unique rights of relationship with his wife are well known. It would be pointless to try to prove what every husband jealously guards. So nobody who usurps this right can claim ignorance of what he is doing. Seducing another man's wife is the worst theft of all. In this one injustice there is a whole heap of wrongs; some towards the woman, and some towards the other man.

It is injustice to the woman's soul, robbing her of her innocence. It's setting her on a course of detestable evil – lust and dishonesty rolled into one. And she may never find the way out again; then the results would be eternal. It brings her public discredit, reproach and disparagement. It deprives her of the happiness which comes from mutual love and affection between husband and wife, bringing loathing and abhorrence to a relationship, and a multitude of other troubles in their wake.

And it's injustice to the husband because it robs him of everything that he counts most precious. The love and faithfulness of his wife are irreplaceable because he must not find them elsewhere even if he wants to. It's impossible without grievously wronging him to take these possessions away. It places the husband in the tormenting pain of jealousy, it drives him to desperate acts, and it brings upon him the scorn and contempt of the world around. Whilst it's true that other people would be wrong to reproach him, yet until the world is changed that's just what will happen. All these side-effects add to the injury.

Adultery is such wanton revelry; for the man who commits it never intends to provide for the other's children, yet defrauds them of so much. So whoever has committed this sin cannot repent of it effectively without restoring to the family as much as he has taken from it.

It really is a sin which can never be put right. In the Jewish law, while the thief was to restore four times as much as he'd taken, the adulterer had no possibility of making restitution and must pay with his life for the offence.

If a man commits adultery with the wife of a fellow-Israelite, both he and the woman shall be put to death. (Leviticus 20.10)

Though these days adulterers fare better and live on to repeat their immorality – even to laugh at those they have injured, let them know that the day of reckoning will come sooner or later, whether they repent or not. If they don't repent, they will find adultery to be a very expensive indulgence – it will cost them much remorse, much fear, much disturbance of conscience, many tears. And even if their whole life could be spent in penitential exercises it would hardly be enough to match the guilt of one single act of this kind. How then about those who indulge in it constantly? However secretly you commit this sin, even though you may think 'no one saw me' (Job 24.15), yet God sees. And it's he who explicity threatens to punish this sort of offence.

Marriage is to be honoured by all, and husbands and wives must be faithful to each other. God will judge those who are immoral and those who commit adultery! (Hebrews 13.4)

OTHERS' POSSESSIONS

We have a duty to let our neighbour enjoy his possessions without seeking to defraud him, or spoil what he has. Anyone who is malicious and bears a grudge against his neighbour, sins against him by trying to spoil what he has. It is a hellish pleasure so to spite someone, reflecting the devil's humour who loves to ruin other people. God didn't allow the Hebrews even to destroy the goods of an enemy:

> If you happen to see your enemy's cow or donkey running loose, take it back to him. If his donkey has fallen under its load, help him to get the donkey to its feet again; don't just walk off. (Exodus 23.4,5)

Logically, then, if we owe it to our enemies to help them, what an injustice it is when we deliberately damage our neighbour's possessions.

There are various ways of attacking our neighbour's property and possessions. We can pervert or corrupt justice by bribes and extortion; in other words, misusing law which was intended for the protection and defence of people's rights, not for their overthrow. There is a very heavy guilt here both on the perpetrator, and on the lawyer who pleads his cause thereby compounding the felony.

Sometimes the circumstantial needs of the oppressed become the means of oppression. So it is with extortion and financial exploitation; a man can be in an extreme need of money and this gives opportunity to the creditor to charge him very high interest. The victim is forced to comply in order to supply his needs. It is the same where an unprincipled landlord has a tenant who has no opportunity to avoid an extortionate rent. The more helpless the victim, the more heinous the crime. Hence Scripture's pronouncement on the oppressor of widow and orphan:

> He cheats the poor, he robs, he keeps what a borrower gives him as security...he lends money for profit. Will he live? No, he will not. He has done all these disgusting things, and so he will die. He will be to blame for his own death! (Ezekiel 18.12,13)

God has taken upon himself the protection of the poor and the oppressed. He is in honour bound to be their avenger. He solemnly declares his purpose to appear for them:

> Now I will come, because the needy are oppressed and the

persecuted groan in pain. I will give them the security they long for. (Psalm 12.5)

So we should take the advice of Proverbs:

Don't take advantage of the poor just because you can; don't take advantage of those who stand helpless in court. The Lord will argue their case for them and threaten the life of anyone who threatens theirs. (Proverbs 22.22,23)

If it is God's intention to intervene, there will be little pleasure in exploiting the poor.

OTHERS' RIGHTS

There are two types of stealing; one is taking something from someone else, and the other is withholding what we owe. Anything we owe by duty or by our own voluntary promise is a debt. Withholding debts has nowadays become common practice. It doesn't seem to matter how much the creditor has to waste his time and set aside other business in order to chase the debtor. So the creditor becomes a loser twice over. I just can't see how a man can look on anything that he possesses as his own while he denies somebody else what is rightly theirs. Rather than ruin his neighbour he ought to sell everything he has and rely upon God's provision. That course of action would bring blessing, in place of the debtor's curse.

Anyone who defers paying his debts will in the end be made to do it by law, and with interest – probably on much worse terms than he could have done it voluntarily. He'll also lose his reputation, and when he needs to borrow again no-one will want to lend to him. The sure way of avoiding this sort of trouble is never to borrow more than you know you have the means to repay, unless you're conscious of your liability and you're willing to take the risk. If you do over-borrow, you commit a sin at the outset, because you take from your neighbour on promise of payment more than you can ever give him back – and that's robbery.

The same principles of justice which apply to the debtor also affect those who stand surety for others. If you guarantee someone else's debt, you make it your own. You may think it hard that you should end up paying for something from which you never received any benefit. It *is* hard, and that should warn you to be careful of making any such agreement; but it can't be an excuse for breaking your agreement.

If you've promised something, it's an injustice if you withhold it. Once you have promised it, it becomes the other person's right. The just man,

> always does what he promises, no matter how much it may cost. (Psalm 15.4)

And from Psalm 15.1 we deduce that anyone who does not keep this kind of promise on time is fit neither for worship here nor for heaven hereafter.

If you are an employer you may consider the wages you pay to be this kind of promissory debt. Withholding wages is sin and God knows about it:

> You have not paid any wages to the men who work in your fields, listen to their complaints! The cries of those who gather in your crops have reached the ears of God, the Lord Almighty. (James 5.4)

The Old Testament legal code has strict instructions on this matter:

> Do not cheat a poor and needy hired servant, whether he is a fellow-Israelite or a foreigner living in one of your towns. Each day before sunset pay him for that day's work; he needs the money and has counted on getting it. If you do not pay him, he will cry out against you to the Lord, and you will be guilty of sin. (Deuteronomy 24.14,15)

The sin is one that shouts aloud and will not stop – until God's vengeance comes down on you. So even if you have no sense of justice as far as your brother is concerned, yet at least have mercy on yourself and avoid the inevitable judgement that will fall on you for so wronging him.

HONESTY

There are two main ways of stealing: violently and openly, or secretly and in an underhand manner. Some take by force, others by petty pilfering. I'm not going to argue which of these is worse, it's enough to know that they are both unjust acts; they make men unacceptable to God and unfit for human society. Inevitably, most thieves are caught and punished. It's stupid for anyone to think that he can always get away with it, for he's up against the energy and intelligence of those he steals from. The more they lose, the more they will apply themselves to discovering him. What is far more perilous for the thief is struggling against the justice of God which usually hounds such men to their own downfall in this world. And even if there were no danger here, there's every danger in the world to come. He can only save himself from that consequence if he repents and reforms. So, when we weigh up these dangers it's a poor bargain: you steal your neighbour's money or property and in exchange you pay with your freedom or your soul – perhaps both! Jesus said having the whole world was too cheap a price for losing your soul (Mark 8.36), and he knows the value of souls for he has bought them himself. If that is so, how stupid it is to sell your soul – as many do that get into the habit of stealing – for any petty thing that catches your eye!

Receiving stolen goods is just as bad as stealing. Many who pretend disgust at stealing are only too willing to buy something a little cheaper when it's been stolen by someone else. And if you conceal something which you know belongs to someone else then you are guilty too. The kind of person who does this would probably commit the grosser offence of outright robbery if he were not in danger from the law.

There are various kinds of deceit, but two general divisions would be these: deceit in a matter of trust, and deceit in matters of trade. I suppose I should add deceit in gambling, which is as much a fraud as any of the rest.

If some trust is committed to you and you deceive the one who has trusted you and fail the trust, you are committing two sins at once: you are defrauding him and breaking your promise to him. In every trust there is a promise implicit if not explicit, for in accepting a trust you make a promise of faithfulness. Trusts of various sorts can be broken – sometimes to the living, sometimes to the dead. May be the trust is in the form of a legacy, or it may be simply a delegation of responsibility. In our work we may be responsible for someone else's property. In all these things you can betray a trust by not acting with the same scrupulousness that you would for yourself. If you are careless and lose the goods that are entrusted to you, or if you deliberately embezzle or convert them to your own use, you betray the trust. Similarly, if you are trustee of some money or property under the terms of a legacy: if you don't fulfil the terms and distribute the property according to the intention of the dead person, if you enrich yourself by what is left for others, you are guilty of betrayal. In fact you are more guilty if you sin against the dead than you would be if you sinned against the living, for the dead have no remedy or redress. It is just like robbing a grave – an act for which people have great distaste and horror. You would have to be a very hardened thief to attempt that.

This kind of sin is much worse when property or money is left to God, or the poor, or charity. By diverting such money or goods you add sacrilege to your fraud and treachery. So heavy are the penalties that you may get a very bad bargain!

FAIR TRADING

In trade, both seller and buyer can be deceitful. The seller might conceal the faults of his commodity, or else over-rate it. To conceal the fault, he would either have to tell an outright lie – adding this sin to the other; or he might confirm the lie with an oath adding the guilt of perjury too. See how one sin gets piled upon another! Enough to submerge any weak person in hell – and all this just to make a little more money.

Another way of concealing the faults in your goods is by making them look more attractive than they merit. This is *acting* a lie even though it's not *telling* one – which amounts to the same thing in the end.

A third way of deceit in trade is to make sure that purchasers don't really know the good from the bad; that is, trading on their ignorance. If you wish to trade justly you must let the purchaser know what he's buying. If he doesn't know enough about the goods you are selling, you are bound to tell him. Otherwise you are making him pay for something which isn't there. He is assuming that it is of good quality and you know differently. You might as well be selling him something that you haven't got – and anyone would admit that was cheating.

Then there's the kind of 'weights and measures' deceit of concealing the deficiencies in *quantity*. Again this is making the purchaser pay for something which he doesn't get.

The Lord hates people who use dishonest scales. He is happy with honest weights. (Proverbs 11.1)

It's just as fraudulent for the seller to over-rate the *quality* of the thing he is selling. Even though he hasn't disguised its faults and has dealt fairly in that respect, yet if he puts an unreasonable price on it he still defrauds the buyer. What I call an unreasonable price is one which exceeds the true worth of a thing when you have taken a moderate profit into account. Anything over and above this can only be got by taking advantage of the purchaser's ignorance of the value of the thing, or of his need for the item. For surely the purchaser's need for something can't have any affect on what you have paid for it. It's an unethical way of trading simply to rate things higher and higher because your neighbour's need increases.

It's quite possible to take advantage of the purchaser's lack of restraint. He may set his heart on something and let his desire over-rule his logic so that he wants it on any terms. If you become aware of this and put the price up because of it, you are making him buy his own foolishness. Because he fancies the object, that doesn't add anything to its real value and therefore shouldn't add anything to the price. So if you want to deal fairly in selling you must not grab at every advantage which the temperament of the customer may give, but you should decide objectively what the thing is worth; what you would sell it for to someone else of whom you couldn't take advantage, and so fix your price for the customer.

From the buyer's point of view there are not so many opportunities to be deceitful. Yet, as sometimes happens, a man may sell something to you without being aware of the true worth. It's not right that you should profit by his ignorance. More often, a seller's need compels him to part with something, and the buyer tries to force him down. That is unjust too.

In trade there are so many opportunities for deceit that you have to be very strong-minded to resist them. More than that, you need a love for truth and justice in order not to fall into temptation.

> How hard it is for a merchant to keep clear of wrong, or for a shop-keeper to be innocent of dishonesty! Many have cheated for gain; a money-grabber will always turn a blind eye. As a peg is held fast in the joint between stones, so dishonesty squeezes in between selling and buying. Unless a man holds resolutely to the fear of the Lord, his house will soon be in ruins. (Ecclesiasticus 27.1-3)

The problem is that these refined forms of deceit are taught as the art of trading. It has all become part of the job, so that unless you have some skill in deception you are unlikely to make the grade. Those who trade like this congratulate themselves and tell others how they have exploited their neighbours.

It is a disgrace that Christians, bound by their faith to the high duty of love, should behave instead against the common rules of natural justice, bring shame on the name of Christ and reproach from others. What we have learnt here should be enough to persuade us to change.

From the Old Testament writings come some warnings of the consequences of deceit and oppression;

> If you make gifts to rich people or oppress the poor to get rich, you will become poor yourself. (Proverbs 22.16)

> You take what isn't yours, but you are doomed! How long will you go on getting rich by forcing your debtors to pay up? Before you know it, you that have conquered others will be in debt yourselves and be forced to pay interest. (Habakkuk 2.6,7)

It's often the way with those who deprive and cheat others that in the end somebody else does the same thing to them. Zechariah's vision shows God's attitude to this sin:

> I looked again, and this time I saw a scroll flying through the air; the angel asked me what I saw. I answered, 'A scroll flying through the air; it is nine metres long and four and a half metres wide.' Then he said to me, 'On it is written the curse that is going to go over the whole land. On one side of the scroll it says that every thief will be removed from the land; and on the other side it says that everyone who tells lies under oath will also be taken away. The Lord Almighty says that he will send this curse out, and it will enter the house of every thief and the house of everyone who tells lies under oath. It will remain in their houses and leave them in ruins.' (Zechariah 5.1-4)

Notice that theft and perjury – stealing and lying – are the two sins which this passage condemns (sins which so often go together); and that God's vengeance for them is the destruction of the 'houses' of those who perjure. So, in effect, when you are scouting around to pilfer your neighbour's goods or his home, you are really gathering fuel to burn your own! And we often see what happens to those who have got their wealth by foul means: they themselves go to bankrupt.

MAKING RESTITUTION

Even if you are sure that the things you have gained unjustly will be not taken away from you, you shouldn't forget how dearly you will have to pay for them in another world. You have little cause to boast of your prize. You may think that you have been very clever and got one over your brother, but all the while there has been somebody else cheating you out of something infinitely more precious – your soul. It is the devil. He uses you as a fisherman uses bait. He wants to catch you – the big fish – and he baits the hook with a small one. So while you're gaping wide to swallow up your poor brother, you yourself become a victim to the devil. Of course, your ill-gotten wealth won't be any consolation to you in hell since you will have left it behind on earth. Think about this and resolve from now on to use all the energy and cunning that you have employed to deceive others to rescue yourself from the tricks of the great deceiver.

This is why it's absolutely necessary that you should pay back all those whom you have defrauded. For as long as you keep anything you have stolen you hold it as a deposit from the devil which gives him eventual right to your soul.

What happens then if it's not possible to make restitution? If the person you have wronged is dead, for instance? Well, in that case pay what you owe to his heirs. What happens if you can't remember whom you have defrauded? The only advice that I can give is that you should try as hard as you can to remember who it was, and discover where they are. If after all this it proves impossible to find out, then pay the money over to charity and make such that you get rid of every last coin.

Even this may not be possible because you may not have kept account of what you have gained unjustly. For example a tradesman couldn't tell how much he had cheated in every single parcel but he could probably guess the gross value or the pecentage he had taken. So let him work out how much he owes and pay it. He must deal honestly – with God watching him, he shouldn't keep anything back because he has forgotten how much he took! If he is not sure, he should give more rather than less.

Making restitution is not easy, and the more we realise it, the more careful we shall be not to deal unjustly. Basically, it's our covetousness – envy – that we have to deal with; this is the root of the evil.

GUARDING REPUTATIONS

Part of the responsibility of justice concerns our neighbours' reputation. Under no circumstance are we to harm their character or to destroy their good name. In particular, we are not to slander our neighbours.

There are two ways of telling untruths about people. The first is when we say something which we know to be false, the second is when we suggest something harmful to their reputation on the basis of guess-work, or simply conjecture arising from jealousy; when the grounds for what we say are so uncertain that our facts are as likely to be false as true. It's clear that if you lie about someone you are guilty of sin. Everybody acknowledges that it's a dastardly thing to tell lies about other people and bring them into disrepute. But you're just as responsible if you report as a certainty or even as a probability something of which you're not absolutely sure. By this you rob your neighbour of his good reputation. People are always willing to believe the worst of others and the slightest suggestion will at once be spread around. It really is a most intolerable injustice that people should spread evil rumours on slight evidence, chancing what calamity they might bring on the subject of their gossip. Usually such rumours spring from some-one's condemning attitude or ill-will, rather than from any real fault in the victim of their gossip.

False reports come both by the shout and by the whisper. Many times people perjure themselves in the courts; this not only hurts the victim's reputation, but also brings unjust punishment upon him through the process of law, the degree of punishment depend-ing on the crime of which he is accused. If the alleged crime is murder it may put his life at risk. (See what happened to Naboth in 1 Kings 21.)

The ninth commandment says, 'Do not accuse anyone falsely' (Exodus 20.16; Deuteronomy 5.20). In the Old Testament law, the slanderer was to receive as punishment what he was trying to bring upon his victim:

> If one man tries to harm another by falsely accusing him of a crime, both are to go to the one place of worship and be judged by the priests and judges who are then in office. The judges will investigate the case thoroughly; and if the man has made a false accusation against his fellow-Israelite, he is to receive the punishment the accused man would have received. (Deuteronomy 19.16-19)

False reports don't only occur in court or before a magistrate, they may happen in other company; worst of all in company which is likely to carry the rumour further. Such reports are usually made with bitterness and vituperance. It's part of the art of slanderers to speak hatefully of those they slander in order to sharpen their accusation in the minds of their hearers. This wicked sin of telling evil lies about somebody will keep us out of heaven:

Lord, who may enter your temple?
  Who may worship on Zion, your sacred hill?
A person who obeys God in everything
  and always does what is right,
whose words are true and sincere,
  and who does not slander others.
He does no wrong to his friends
  and does not spread rumours about his neighbours.

(Psalm 15.1-3)

St Paul tells us that those who commit this sin should be kept from the church's fellowship too (1 Corinthians 5.11), and they will not possess God's kingdom (1 Corinthians 6.10).

Then there is the other sort of a rumour-monger, the whisperer. He goes from one person to another and privately tells his story. It is not really his intention to keep the scandal a secret, but rather to make it more so. This trick of passing out the story as a confidence is his way of getting it believed and talked about. For those who are told something in secret know they can please somebody else by passing on the secret. So it is that the story passes from one to another until at last it spreads thoughout a whole town. Of all slanderers, this type is the most dangerous. He works in the dark; he warns everyone he speaks to not to say who has told them. Whereas with public accusation the victim may have some opportunity to reply and so clear himself, with the secret rumour he has no chance at all. The secret slander, like undetectable poison, works its incurable evil before anybody discovers it. St Paul names the sin of evil gossip among those crimes which come from a corrupted mind (Romans 1.29).

Gossip is a wound and disease of human society. It not only robs individuals of their good name, but often families, groups of people, of their peace.

Evil people look for ways to harm others; even their words burn with evil. Gossip is spread by wicked people; they stir up trouble and break up friendship. (Proverbs 16.27,28)

And of those who behave this way, St. James says,

Their tongues are set on fire by hell. (James 3.6)

This is a dangerous sin. Here's how to fall right into it:

First step: listen to, and encourage those who come to you with gossip. As the old proverb says: 'If there were no receiver of stolen goods, there would no thief.' So if no-one listened to tittle-tattle, there wouldn't by any tale-bearers.

Second step: believe easily what you hear! Slanderers want you to think badly of their victim, but you do him great injustice if you believe in his guilt without good grounds. Stories coming from people like this are not worth taking notice of.

Third step: pass on to others what you have been told. That makes you party to the lie, so there's not much between you and the person who told it in the first place.

One step leads to another. You must keep your innocence from the beginning, and not countenance any false report. Once you become open to this sort of gossip you will never have peace again because you'll always be open to persuasion about other people, stirring up trouble even among your own relatives. So, you see, a gossip and a slanderer is to be looked upon as the common enemy; the enemy of those he speaks to as well as those he speaks about.

We must not show contempt or despise other people. Making jokes at their expense, and running them down in public, is wrong. Such behaviour harms people's reputation; for, by and large, people base their opinions on trust rather than on judgement. If they see someone derided and looked down upon, they are likely to do the same themselves.

These are the four things that people cruelly exploit:

1. A person's goodness and godliness.

2. A natural weakness.

3. A misfortune – something that has happened to him.

4. A misdemeanour – something he has done wrong.

If someone is deformed, ugly, or mentally retarded, these are things beyond his control. They are not his fault but are allowed by God who gives beauty and intelligence to whom he pleases. So if we despise someone because he hasn't got these qualities, we reproach God.

In the same way God's providence permits misfortune – whether it's illness or anything else. It's not for us to judge what his motives are. So if someone is sick we are not to conclude that they are also guilty. Many people do this without any evidence. Jesus reproves the Jews for jumping to conclusions, and he gave as an example the Galileans whom Pilate killed while they were offering sacrifices to God:

Jesus answered them, 'Because those Galileans were killed in that way, do you think that it proves that they were worse sinners than all the other Galileans? No indeed!' (Luke 13.2,3)

When we see God's hand lying heavy upon other people it's not our business to judge them. We should judge ourselves and repent, to avoid what our own sins rightly deserve. Those who reproach and mock other people in trouble are guilty of savage cruelty and the height of wickedness:

They persecute those whom you have punished; they talk about sufferings of those you have wounded. Keep a record of all their sins; don't let them have any part in your salvation. May their names be erased from the book of the living. May they not be included in the list of your people. (Psalm 69.26-28)

Even when other people *sin*, though they seem to deserve our reproach, we are to be very compassionate. We must never forget how easily we could be in their place. It's only by God's mercy that we are preserved from the worst that can happen to anybody else. So the thing to do is to look up to God with thankfulness, rather than down on the fellow-sinner with contempt.

It is very difficult to restore someone's good name when you have taken it away. It is a thing that he holds most precious – sometimes even dearer than his life, as we see by the dangers people face in order to prove their qualities. And this good name is considered by wise people one of the greatest happinesses of life. For people in some occupations a good reputation is absolutely essential. You might as well say that they depend on their reputation for their living. So, you see, it's no light matter to rob a man of what is so valuable to him.

If you damage someone's reputation, it is very difficult to put things right afterwards. Perhaps I should say that it's nearer impossible than difficult. For once people are persuaded ill of someone, there's no changing their minds. Even if people were as willing to believe good as they are to believe ill of their neighbours, the one who wanted to set a slander right would never know if he would be heard by everybody who believed his story the first time.

This should deter you from so wronging your neighbour. But if it's too late and you have already fallen into this sin, that's no excuse for not doing what you can to put it right. What is more, if it can't be set right without bringing public shame upon yourself through your confession of guilt, yet that is what you must do however great the cost.

Let me summarise what I have said so far about doing right by our neighbour. We must love not only with our words and actions, but with our thoughts and feelings too. Not only must we refrain from hurting our neighbour, we must also refrain from hating him. We must never wish our neighbour ill or be pleased about accidents that happen to him. We must not envy him what he possesses, or wish to live the life he lives. Not only must we refrain from saying anything evil about him, we must clear our minds of wishing him ill. And we must not rejoice at evil done to him. Do you see that while man's laws cover words and actions, God's laws reach the heart and mind? The reason is clear: the great Judge of all can see heart and mind too.

Be careful how you think; your life is shaped by your thoughts. Never say anything which isn't true. Have nothing to do with lies and misleading words. (Proverbs 4.23,24)

We have to keep a very careful watch on our minds – that nothing wrong or unjust enters – not only to stop us doing unjust things but also to keep ourselves unpolluted in God's sight. Only if our hearts are pure shall we see God clearly:

Happy are the pure in heart; they will see God! (Matthew 5.8)

TRUTHFULNESS

Let's now talk about the positive acts of justice which form part of our duty to our neighbour.

Speaking the truth – this we owe to everybody. Speech is given to us by God so that we can talk to each other and discover each other's minds and know each other's friendship. It is a gift given to us for the advantage of everyone, and it must be used for that purpose. The liar uses speech to injure those he speaks to.

I could say a lot about how important it is to tell the truth, but since I'm writing for Christians I need not go any further than the principles of the Bible.

No more lying, then! Everyone must tell the truth to his fellow-believer, because we are all members together in the body of Christ. (Ephesians 4.25)

Do not lie to one another, for you have taken off the old self with its habits and have put on the new self. (Colossians 3.9,10)

There are seven things that the Lord hates and cannot tolerate: a proud look, a lying tongue, hands that kill innocent people, a mind that thinks up wicked plans, feet that hurry off to do evil, a witness who tells one lie after another, and a man who stirs up trouble among friends. (Proverbs 6.16-19)

See how much God hates lies! We must not lie even in an enthusiasm to promote God's glory, our zeal is no excuse for telling untruths:

What if my untruth serves God's glory by making his truth stand out more clearly? Why should I still be condemned as a sinner? Why not say, then, 'Let us do evil so that good may come'? (Romans 3.7,8)

If it is damnable to lie in the cause of religion what will happen to those who lie for other reasons? Some lie maliciously, intending to hurt others; some lie through envy, intending to steal from others; some lie from pride, simply to show off; and some out of fear, to avoid danger or to stop people finding out the truth about them. But the oddest thing of all is the lie that is told for no apparent reason. The person who enjoys telling incredible stories gains nothing from it except the reputation of being a provocative liar. Remember...

Lord, who may enter your temple?
    Who may worship on Zion, your sacred hill?
A person who obeys God in everything
    and always does what is right,
whose words are true and sincere,
    and who does not slander others,
he does no wrong to his friends
    and does not spread rumours about his neighbours.'
(Psalm 15.1-3)

Honesty has become such a rarity that it's not easy to find some-body like this. People have got into the habit of telling untruths and do it quite casually, thinking that nobody notices them – not even God. But they are quite wrong; there's hardly any sin which is more difficult to hide – even from other people – than lying. Those who are in the habit of telling lies inevitably slip up and give themselves away, however good their memories are.

Nothing brings greater scorn from other people than persistent lying. To be a liar is a very shameful thing. And as for God not seeing, it's quite stupid to think that all our cleverness can hide such a thing from him. He doesn't need our slips of the tongue to find out that we are telling a lie, because he sees our hearts. He knows that what we are saying is not true from the moment we open our mouths. He is the God of truth and must punish untruth. Have you noticed that when the book 'Revelation' describes the city of God, liars are among those who are shut out? (Revelation 22.15)

COURTESY

The character Nabal in 1 Samuel (25.17) was so pig-headed that he wouldn't listen to anybody! This is not the Christian way. We must respect other people's right to an opinion. It doesn't matter what our position in life is – by accident of birth or wealth or position; no such advantage can excuse us from politeness even to the most lowly person. So that anyone who is harsh or arrogant to other people offends against his own human nature. And when we add to this the dignity conferred upon mankind by the Son of God, who took all humanity upon himself, our duty of respect for others becomes all the greater, and our failure to show respect all the more contemptible.

People who are proud and self-confident become so busy admiring themselves that they take no notice of what is valuable in other people. They refuse to be civil to others, yet they set themselves up – as Nebuchadnezzar set up the statue of himself (Daniel 3.1-7) – to be worshipped by everyone. But St Paul says:

Be eager to show respect for one another. (Romans 12.10)

Don't do anything from selfish ambition or from a cheap desire to boast, but be humble towards one another, always considering others better than yourselves. (Philippians 2.3)

And Luke's Gospel reminds us of the words of Jesus:

Everyone who makes himself great will be humbled, and everyone who humbles himself will be made great. (Luke 14.11)

PATIENCE

A further duty to others is patience and gentleness. We must tame anger. It not only damages our own character but has hurtful effects on others – witness the many atrocities committed against children through loss of temper.

Be patient with everyone. See that no one pays back wrong for wrong, but at all times make it your aim to do good to one another and to all people. (1 Thessalonians 5.14,15)

Paul urges Timothy to be patient and gentle even with those who oppose his Christian teaching – and surely if God were going to allow us to get cross about anything it would be about this sort of thing:

> The Lord's servant must not quarrel. He must be kind towards all, a good and patient teacher who is gentle as he corrects his opponents, for it may be that God will give them the opportunity to repent and come to know the truth. (2 Timothy 2.24,25)

The peace of the world depends on this virtue of patience and gentleness. It's no small wonder then that Christ who came to plant peace amongst us should tell us to be peaceable. I'm sure you can see everywhere the ill effects of anger and bad temper. Anger breeds unrest – in the nation, in the neighbourhood, in the family, and even between man and wife. Proverbs tells us never to make friends with a bad tempered person:

> Don't make friends with people who have hot, violent tempers. You might learn their habits and not be able to change. (Proverbs 22.24)

Bad temper makes a person unfit to live with:

> Better to live out in the desert than with a nagging, complaining wife. (Proverbs 21.19)

St Matthew sets out what Jesus says about anger in a whole paragraph in Matthew 5.21-26. Here Jesus tells us the danger we are in if we call someone else an idiot. But every day we do worse than that – with many terms of abuse which we use when we lose our temper.

Worse still we sometimes turn our harsh criticisms into curses. How often do we hear people swearing at others – for the slightest cause, perhaps without any cause at all? It just shows how completely we've forgotten St Paul's rule,

> Ask God to bless those who persecute you – yes ask him to bless, not to curse. (Romans 12.14)

And it shows how completely we have forgotten that Jesus said,

> I tell you: love your enemies and pray for those who persecute you, so that you may become the sons of your Father in Heaven. (Matthew 5.44,45)

Cursing is the language of hell and never should be found on the lips of inhabitants of the City of God.

> Get rid of all bitterness, passion, and anger. No more shouting or insults, no more hateful feelings of any sort. (Ephesians 4.31)

RESPECT

God bestows special gifts on some people. We must willingly and gladly acknowledge these gifts and show our respect to the people concerned. We must not, out of a sheer pride in our own gifts, undervalue those of others.

Neither must we envy or begrudge the gifts that other people have. To do so is to wrong them – and also God, who gave the gifts. Remember how Jesus put it, in the parable of Matthew chapter 20: some of the workers grumbled at their employer's generosity to others. And the employer said 'Can't I do what I like with my own money? Because I am kind, should you be unkind?' So, when we envy God's goodness to others, we are in effect grumbling against God who distributed his gifts like this. Surely there can be nothing worse than to hate and wish ill to somebody else for no other reason than that God has loved him and been kind to him.

Don't disparage other people's good points. It's usually jealousy that's at the root of this. If you are jealous of someone, you will do all you can to lessen people's opinions of him. If you can't play down the good things about him, you'll try and persuade others of some real or pretended weakness. This is wrong and quite opposite to our Christian obligation to acknowledge and to show respect for the gifts God has given to others.

Both these sins – envying other people and detracting from their goodness – usually prove as foolish as they are wicked. For jealousy brings constant pain and self-torture. If you could only be happier about the other person's gifts it would enrich your own experience – you'd enjoy being pleased for him. Besides which the other person's gifts may be of great advantage to you. His common sense, his understanding, his education could teach you much; his faith and goodness could be a helpful example to you. But if you are envious you lose all this and you gain nothing except a constant headache! You'll fret about it and let if eat away at your heart.

What's more, people will soon find out what your game is. You can't forever run down the virtuous without being found out. The net result will be that you fall in everyone's estimation.

All that I have said about the respect due to those who have spiritual and mental gifts and qualities may in a lesser degree be applied to those who have the external advantages of honour and greatness. These things are not as important as the others, yet ranks and distinctions are permitted by God. By them the world is governed. So we must have a respect for civil authority. In general, all juniors must respect their seniors. If we are rebellious and impertinent we only contradict the order which God has placed in the world.

GENEROSITY

I want to talk of our obligation to those in need and poverty. If someone is in distress and needs something and I can supply that thing, then there is an obligation upon me to bring him what he needs. The logic of this is that God has given us our abilities not only for our own use but for the advantage and benefit of others. Let's see the application of this . . .

1. If anyone lacks knowledge we are to instruct them:

    The Lord God has given me the voice of a teacher so that I can strengthen the weary. (Isaiah 50.4)

2. If anyone is unhappy or in trouble we are to comfort him, since we are blessed with happiness:

    God helps us in all our troubles, so that we are able to help others who have all kinds of troubles, using the same help that we ourselves have received from God. (2 Corinthians 1.4)

3. If anyone is lost in sin, wants to be helped to reform and needs advice, we must help them – that is if we have opportunity and sufficient ability, and if it is likely that we can do him any good:

    You shall not nurse hatred against your brother. You shall speak to him frankly and rebuke him. In this way you will have no share in his guilt. (Leviticus 19.17)

    Note, we are under obligation to rebuke, not to hate.

4. If a person is being slandered – untruths are being told about him – we are to defend him and help clear his name if we know he is innocent. Otherwise we become guilty of the slander because we have neglected to do anything about it.

5. If we find people in poverty, we must give them relief and charity.

> Do not withhold good from those who deserve it, when it is in your power to act. Do not say to your neighbour, 'Come back later; I'll give it tomorrow' – when you now have it with you. (Proverbs 3.27,28)

Evidently to delay helping our poor neighbour is as bad as to refuse help altogether. God's Old Testament instruction to the Hebrews was that they should take a tenth of their profit every third year – which is a thirtieth every year – and use it for the relief of the poor (Deuteronomy 14.28,29). This was not a matter of charity or generosity but an obligation; they had failed in their duty if they did not 'tithe'. How do we imagine that Christian principles of giving should be so much inferior to those of Judaism that either nothing at all, or a lesser proportion should be required of us? If what we did came anywhere near our duty in this matter then we wouldn't see so many poor and destitute people in the world. To spend the money we owe God on our luxuries is surely nothing short of robbery.

In the five examples above, those to whom God has given gifts and opportunites are to think of themselves as his stewards. They are trustees of what has been put into their hands for passing on to those in need. So then, if we misappropriate those gifts and use them for our own personal benefit, we are stealing – we are quite as bad as a cashier who embezzles his till, or a manager who misappropriates company funds for his own use. Anyone who does this is likely to lose his job. And whoever does this with what God has given him, has just as much reason to expect the loss of his job.

Just as with every other gift, so with wealth – it's very often observed that those who cheat the poor of their dues, lose their own money. And mean people often become poor despite themselves.

The Hebrews used to ask God to bless them:

> Look down from the holy place in heaven and bless your people Israel; bless also the rich and fertile land which you have given us, as you promised our ancestors. (Deuteronomy 26.15)

But first they had to pay their 'tithes':

> Every third year give the tithe – a tenth of your crops – to the Levites, the foreigners, the orphans, and the widows, so that in every community they will have all that they need to eat. (Deuteronomy 26.12)

So, giving comes before blessing:

> Be generous, and you will be prosperous. Help others, and you will be helped. (Proverbs 11.25)

Exactly what relation are we in to those to whom we owe something? The case of the debtor's obligation to the creditor we have already discussed, and the relationship depends on the bargain, loan or promise. On the other side, the creditor is to deal charitably and Christianly with the debtor and not to exact from him more than he is able to pay.

APPRECIATION

If anyone has done good to us, whether it's spiritual good or physical good, we must show our thanks – readily and warm-heartedly – for what they have given us. Then we should pray for God's blessing and God's reward for those who have been good to us. More than that, we should take what opportunites we have of returning their kindnesses.

These duties are quite accepted by people. Jesus said, 'Sinners do good to those who do good to them'. (Luke 6.33) Yet how many of us fail! How often we neglect to repay courtesies – even returning injury instead! It happens in many situations, but none more than the case of advice and warning, the most valuable of all kindnesses – a really good turn that one person can do for another. We should think of those who give us counsel as our great benefactors. But how few people are grateful for advice – they don't even have the patience to listen!

If you go to warn somebody about something that they are doing wrong, or tell them about a mistake they've made, from then on they will look on you as their enemy. As Paul put it in Galatians 4.16, you become an enemy because you have told them the truth. People's hearts are so proud that they can't take being told that there is anything wrong with them. And that applies even if you have no other motive than to help them put it right. It's just as stupid a situation as if a sick man were to lose his temper with the doctor or to imagine that the doctor was insulting him in assuming him to be ill.

> Anyone who loves knowledge wants to be told when he is wrong. It is stupid to hate being corrected. (Proverbs 12.1)

Nothing can be worse than false assurance. There can't be a more unfortunate position than this because it confirms you in your failings and cuts you off from any hope of change for the better. Catastrophe is inevitable.

> If you get more stubborn every time you are corrected, one day you will be crushed, and never recover. (Proverbs 29.1)

And what of the person who is good enough to advise you? He comes to you out of sympathy and kindness, to help you to avoid danger. He gives himself a very difficult job to do. What loss of face he has to suffer, how sad he will be when he finds that instead of helping you to correct the first fault he's become the occasion of another, groundless, resentment! How cruel you are to him!

RULERS

In the sight of God we have three sorts of parent – not only our natural parents, but our civil and spiritual parents. Our civil parent is the head of State – where his (or her) authority is established justly and by God. He is the father of all those who are under his authority, and we owe to him respect and honour. For to him God has delegated his own authority. We should not for any reason 'speak evil of the ruler of our people' (Acts 23.5).

> That is also why you pay taxes, because the authorities are working for God when they fulfil their duties. Pay, then, what you owe them; pay them your personal and property taxes, and show respect and honour for them all. (Romans 13.6,7)

God has put them there, for everyone's good, as his servants. It is only right then that they should be kept and supported by the people. When you think about the pressures and problems of those in authority, there's very little reason to begrudge them their reward. Very few of those they are set over have such a hard time earning their living!

> First of all, then, I urge that petitions, prayers, requests, and thanksgivings be offered to God for all people; for kings and all others who are in authority, that we may live a quiet and peaceful life with all reverence towards God and with proper conduct. (1 Timothy 2.1,2)

These of all people need our prayers – their responsibilities are so heavy, and the dangers to us from mistakes they might make are so great. We should pray for God's leading for them and his help and blessing. Our prayers will be for our own benefit in the long run, if we have a 'quiet and peaceful life'.

> For the sake of the Lord submit to every human authority: to the Emperor, who is the supreme authority, and to the governors, who have been appointed by him to punish the evil-doers and to praise those who do good! (1 Peter 2.13,14)

Our duty is to obey the supreme power and to submit to whoever is authorised by him. St Paul makes this point at length:

> Everyone must obey the State authorities, because no authorities exist without God's permission, and the existing authorities have been put there by God. (Romans 13.1)

The interesting thing is that Paul wrote this at a time when such authorities were heathen and in fact persecuted the Christians. We see, then, that we can't free ourselves of this duty of honour simply by pointing out that our rulers behave badly. Obedience is necessary – active obedience in the case of lawful instructions (lawful for Christians, that is, and not contrary to some commandment of God). Of course, when the civil authority tries to make us do something contrary to the express commandments of God then we should not obey. Then we can – or rather must – resist; we should, 'obey God, not men' (Acts 5.29).

And yet, from a passive point of view, we should still be submissive. If there is punishment for our refusal to obey, then we must accept it without complaint – there must be no revolution. We take David's principle from 1 Samuel:

> David said, 'You must not harm him! The Lord will certainly punish whoever harms his chosen king. By the living Lord,' David continued, 'I know that the Lord himself will kill Saul either when his time comes to die a natural death or when he dies in battle. The Lord forbid that I should try to harm the one whom the Lord has made King!' (1 Samuel 26.9-11)

Remember that David was under extreme provocation from Saul, and also was certain to succeed him – yet he spoke like this. St Paul adds his voice to the argument, with strong words,

> Whoever opposes the existing authority opposes what God has ordered; and anyone who does so will bring judgement on himself. (Romans 13.2)

Remember that even those who revolt aginst lawful authority here, one day have to face the supreme authority of God – and there is no hiding from him. Remember too, that it's quite beside the point for us to protest, 'Those in authority don't do their duty so why should we do ours?' Most of them know what their duties are and they are accountable to God for their own failures. In other words, their failings can be no excuse for ours.

MINISTERS

Ministers of the word of God are our spiritual parents. Whether church leaders or pastors, it is their duty to do for our souls what our natural parents do for our bodies. Let me illustrate by reference to some of St Paul's descriptions:

> In your life in union with Christ Jesus I have become your father by bringing the good news to you. (1 Corinthians 4.15)

> Once again, just like a mother in childbirth, I feel the same kind of pain for you until Christ's nature is formed in you. (Galatians 4.19)

> I had to feed you with milk, not with solid food, beause you were not ready for it. (1 Corinthians 3.2; see also Hebrews 5.14)

Our duty to our spiritual parents is first to love them – to be as kind to them as we ought to, considering the great blessing they bring us.

> We beg you, our brothers, to pay proper respect to those who work among you, who guide and instruct you in the Christian life. Treat them with the greatest respect and love because of the work they do. (1 Thessalonians 5.12,13)

Don't we respect people of other jobs and professions according to what they do? Well, there can be no commodity as precious as a soul, and these are the Chrisitian minister's stock in trade. He rescues valuable souls from destruction. Then again if we stop to think who employs him, we will have even more respect for him. He is 'Christ's ambassador' (2 Corinthians 5.20). By international custom, ambassadors are treated with the same deference that would be accorded to those who sent them. So Jesus tells his disciples,

> Whoever rejects you rejects me; and whoever rejects me rejects the one who sent me. (Luke 10.16)

Let those who think that deriding the minister's calling is good entertainment remember this: despising an ambassador of Christ is despising both Christ and God himself.

Those who pretend to the ministry without lawful calling, let them be warned too. It's just as if someone went and appointed himself as ambassador from his own head of state. Although the Jewish priests were inferior to ministers of the gospel, yet the writer to the Hebrews says of them:

> No one chooses for himself the honour of being a high priest. It is only by God's call that a man is made high priest – just as Aaron was. (Hebrews 5.4)

What presumption it is for someone to assume this great honour when they haven't been called to it! It's just not good enough for them to say they have an inward call of the Holy Spirit. For God has established an order in the church for admitting men to the ministry, and if anyone takes it on himself without being given proper authority, he sets aside this provision of God. He becomes one of the 'thieves and robbers' of which Jesus speaks (John 10.8). In any case experience shows that some who claim to have an inward call of the Holy Spirit are in fact called by some spirit other than God's. The doctrines they proclaim are often diametrically opposed to the teaching of the Bible – on which all true doctrines must be based.

We have enough warnings against self-appointed instructors in the letters of the apostles, for instance in 2 Timothy 3 and 1 Peter 2. If you condone what they do or attach yourself to them you share in their guilt. For without your encouragement they wouldn't carry on for very long. If you encourage them you are guilty of despising your true pastors. It's happening too much these days. Let's pray that God will be merciful and convict us of this carelessness in time to put a stop to the confusion and ungodliness which comes in so easily when we follow self-appointed teachers.

I have already spoken of our duty to give material and financial support to our ministers. Now let me instruct you to obey them:

> Obey your leaders and follow their orders. They watch over your souls without resting, since they must give God an account of their service. If you obey them, they will do their work gladly; if not they will do it with sadness, and that would be of no help to you. (Hebrews 13.17)

I'm talking about spiritual obedience. That is, whatever they tell us from God's word, we must treat as God's commands and carefully obey, remembering that it is not the minister but God who is asking us to do it. This applies whether the instruction comes in a sermon or in private conversation. In both cases, so long as they keep to the word of God, the ministers are the messengers of God. It is your responsibility to make their task an easy one. Nor must you hurt them by rejecting what they say, for that is a most unkind return for all their care and work.

Remember that it is to your own advantage to obey your ministers in spiritual things, for if you don't you lose the glorious rewards that God offers those who obey his word. There's a sense in which the one who knows and rejects what he knows, is more guilty than the one who never heard (compare John 15.24). So it is if you resist the word of God through your minister.

Finally, we must pray. Paul reminds the Ephesians to pray for all God's people, and adds:

> Pray also for me, that God will give me a message when I am ready to speak, so that I may speak boldly and make known the gospel's secret. (Ephesians 6.19)

> Pray also for us, so that God will give us a good opportunity to preach his message about the secret of Christ. (Colossians 4.3)

So we must pray for our spiritual fathers – that God's Spirit will help them to serve him well in their holy calling.

PARENTS

The third kind of parent is more obvious – our natural parents, our 'human fathers' (Hebrews 12.9). The first duty we owe them is the duty of respect and honour. We must be humble and polite in our attitude towards them. We are not to look for weaknesses in them in order to criticise them – either openly, or secretly in our thoughts. If they do have faults our job is to cover them up. This is a warning to children who not only find fault with their parents but make up faults that aren't there.

Young people will sometimes be too proud and stupid to take their parents' advice. They will pass off wisdom and experience as senility. They should read Proverbs:

> Listen to your father; without him you would not exist. When you mother is old, show her your appreciation. (Proverbs 23.22)

You could find plenty more texts on the same theme in Proverbs, which shows that even the wisest men thought it necessary for children to listen to their parents' advice. Yet young people of our time think it is clever to neglect – even laugh at – the advice their parents give. Let such young people, if they won't take what I say, listen again to the wise man of Proverbs:

> The eye that mocks a father or scorns a mother's old age will be plucked out by magpies or eaten by the vulture's young. (Proverbs 30.17)

Our duty to love them

Another duty we owe to our natural parent is love. We are to be genuinely kind to them; wanting for them every good thing. Anything we do that upsets them or makes them unhappy must be distasteful to us. When we think what they have done for us we shall realise that this is no more than simple gratitude. Not only were they the means of us coming into the world, but also they fed and looked after us. All parents who know the worries and burdens of bringing up a child will consider the love that child returns as some compensation.

We can express this love in several ways; by being kind, by offering respect, honour and affection. We should gladly and readily do things which might bring them joy and comfort, and carefully avoid upsetting and hurting them. Again, we can express our love by praying for them. As children, the debt we owe to our parents is so great that we can never hope to pay it back by ourselves, so we have to call on God's help; to pray that he will reward the good that our parents have done for us by blessing them. They're unspeakable – those children who instead of praying to heaven, ransack hell for curses to put on their parents – the things they say about them! Do they realise what God has laid down, about such behaviour?

> Whoever reviles his father or mother shall be put to death. (Exodus 21.17)

Yet we hear it every day.

Unfortunately there's something much more common than criticism and open defiance of parents. How many children because they are impatient with their parents' management, or greedy to have their parents possessions, have wished for their deaths? If you find yourself doing this, don't forget that even though other people don't know, God sees the wishes of your heart. He judges you according to what you think, rather than by your public behaviour.

Our duty to honour them

The fifth commandment promises long life as a reward for honouring parents:

> Respect your father and your mother, so that you may live a long time in the land that I am giving you. (Exodus 20.12; Deuteronomy 5.16)

This fifth commandment does not include *obedience* but it is commanded in other places in the Bible:

> Children, it is your Christian duty to obey your parents, for this is the right thing to do. (Ephesians 6.1)

> Children, it is your Christian duty to obey your parents always, for that is what pleases God. (Colossians 3.20)

We must obey our parents in everything unless their instructions go against the commands of God. In that case our duty to God comes first. In other words, if a parent is so evil as to make his child steal or lie or do something against God's law, and the child refuses to obey the parent, then it's not wrong. In fact the child *must* disobey the parent or else he offends against his higher duty which he owes to God his heavenly Father. Yet when such refusal becomes necessary it should be done with care, humility and respect. The parent must see that the refusal to do what is wanted comes from conscience and not through sheer stubborness. The trouble is that children think that they have grown out of obedience as soon as they are too big to be smacked. Such rebelliousness is all too common nowadays.

Young people must consider the wishes of their parents about marriage. They should think of themselves as their parents' possessions, so that without stealing they can't give themselves away. This sort of principle is laid down – for example in Numbers:

> When a young woman still living in her father's house makes a vow to give something, she must do everything that she vowed or promised unless her father raises an objection when he hears about it. But if her father forbids her to fulfil the vow when he hears about it, she is not required to keep it. The Lord will forgive her, because her father refused to let her keep it. (Numbers 30.3-5)

Our duty to care for them

Another duty we have to our parents is to look after them in their need – whatever kind of need or illness it is. They may be afflicted mentally, physically or financially; in every way the child is bound to relieve and help the parents. In the cases of weakness of body and infirmity of mind, we can't doubt our duty to care for them when we remember how in our infancy we received the same benefits from our parents. We had no strength to support ourselves, and no understanding to guide ourselves. Our parents supplied both of these. So, out of simple gratitude, we owe this same kind of help to our parents, if through accident or age they need it.

In the case of financial need we should be motivated not only by the generally accepted principle of helping one's parents but also the teaching of Christ (Mark 7.13). What a shame it is when some children, far from helping their parents, disown them! The child holding an important position, or having become wealthy, now breaks with the parents who are accustomed to more humble ways. In this event, the more prosperous the child becomes, the worse the parents fare. Such pride certainly shouts to God for vengenance.

One thing more: no fault in the parents can be an excuse for the child's neglect of duty. St Peter tells employees to show respect to employers who are difficult as well as to those who are easy to get on with. (1 Peter 2.18) Whatever applies to employers and employees certainly applies to parents and children. Children must do their duty not only by kind and virtuous parents, but also by the most difficult and wayward parent.

CHILDREN

What about the parents' obligations towards the children? First they must feed them and look after them; this care begins from birth and continues until the child is able to sustain himself. This is a duty which nature teaches – even animals have great care and tenderness in looking after their young. That alone would condemn parents who neglect their duty here.

I'm not going to enter into the discussion of whether mothers should or should not breast-feed their children, because there can be no general rule. What I would say is that, where there is no disability of sickness, weakness or anything similar, it's surely better for the mother to feed the child herself, because there are so many advantages to the child. A good mother will consider these advantages and they will over-rule any objection she might have on the grounds of inconvenience or fastidiousness; these things can't justify neglect because in themselves they are not sufficient reasons.

But there is another 'first care' of a child which should begin almost as early – it belongs to the child's soul. Parents shouldn't deny them the early blessings of God which baptism conveys. Of course it's not right that we should despair of God's mercy on any children who die before they are baptised, yet it's very wrong of parents to let their children go because of their own neglect.

Educating Children

> Teach a child how he should live, and he will remember it all his life. (Proverbs 22.6)

Parents must provide for the education of their children as soon as children are able to think clearly. First of all, they should be taught about things which affect their eternal happiness. A little at a time they can be taught what God requires of them, and what rewards he has in store for them. Just as jars and tins hold the taste of what's first put in them, so children keep what is taught them from the very beginning. Hence, parents must see that their children are seasoned with goodness and faith. And if parents don't do this there is someone standing by – even from their cots – to fill them with the opposites: bad behaviour and evil.

Another thing: there is so much in our human make-up that inclines to doing wrong rather than right, that children must be watched the whole time in order to stop the devil getting in. The best and only effective way is to help the love of goodness to grow in your child – and the hatred of evil. In this way, when temptations come, children have some defence. It is the responsibility of parents to see to this. To neglect it is cruel.

We consider inhuman those parents who maim or kill their children. We ought to be equally offended when parents neglect their children's moral education and ruin their souls, making them miserable for eternity. There are far too many parents in the world who hand their children over to the devil by default. They fail to tell them soon enough of the ways of God. We know very well that there are many children and young people who are as ignorant of God and Christ as heathens, even though their parents would call themselves Christians. Let such parents be warned that they not only bring misery upon their poor children but guilt on themselves. The principle of responsibility is set out clearly in Ezekiel. God appoints Ezekiel as watchman over Israel, and says to him,

> Mortal man, I am making you a watchman for the nation of Israel. You will pass on to them the warnings I give you. If I announce that an evil man is going to die, but you do not warn him to change his ways so that he can save his life, he will die, still a sinner, and I will hold you responsible for his death. (Ezekiel 3.17,18)

Parents are entrusted by God with the job of guardian over their children; so they have a grave responsibility.

The second part of education is bringing them up to be employable; keeping them busy with some honest work to avoid the devil's great snare of laziness; making sure that they are taught some useful skill so that when they are old enough they may become helpful members of society, and able to make an honest living for themselves.

Correcting Children

Children need encouragement. We should first try to make our children love to do right by giving them incentives. Whenever they do well we should take notice of it, and encourage them to go on. Those parents who think they must always be severe, authoritarian and scolding are quite wrong. St Paul must have this in mind when he says,

> Parents, do not irritate your children or they will become discouraged. (Colossians 3.21)

The certain way of provoking them is to be just as hard and unkind with them when they are good as you are when they do wrong. Paul is right to say that they will then be discouraged and will have no enthusiasm for doing well.

If you have tried every way of persuading and encouraging your children to do right, and it does not work, you will have to scold them. Never use curses or bad language, but speak wisely and sternly. If this fails too, then remember that...

> He who spares the rod hates his son, but he who loves him is careful to discipline him. (Proverbs 13.24)

Those who through indulgence will never smack their children are cruel not kind. For eventually much worse will happen to a child who is left to himself. On the other hand, when you do punish your child it must be in a way that will make the child likely to improve. Punishment has to be given in time – it's no good letting the child go on doing something wrong until the habit has got a hold. Too many parents let their children do what they like (lying, stealing, etc.) without stopping them – even amused to see what they're doing and thinking that it doesn't matter while the children are little. But all the while these vices are taking root, and sometimes the roots are so deep that nothing the parents can do later will ever pull them up.

Correction must be restrained, not exceeding the gravity of the mistake. And it must be appropriate to the tenderness of the child. It must never be administered in anger. If it is, not only will there be a danger of excessive punishment, but also the effect will be lost on the child because he will think he is being corrected not for his faults but because his parent is angry. So he will blame his parent rather than himself. Quite the opposite should be the case, so that the child will be totally aware of what is wrong. Unless the child is aware of what he is doing wrong he will never put it right.

When children are grown up there are still responsibilities for the parent. The parent should observe how the standards of behaviour which they gave to their children in early days are working out in practice. They need to encourage or advise their children, as is appropriate and as opportunity presents itself.

Providing for children

Parents have responsibility for the children's physical needs. Finding them a job is part of this. If God has blessed a parent with wealth, he must in proportion give to his children. Parents must remember that since they were the instruments for bringing their children into the world they must as far as they are able provide for them to live in it comfortably. Those parents who spend to excess on their own enjoyment, not caring what happens to their children and never thinking to provide for them, are most despicable.

Another common fault with parents is this: to defer until after they are dead all provision for their children. Such parents might have great intentions for what they will leave their children in their will but, in the meantime give them little help to live in the world. This has several unfortunate results.

First, it diminishes the child's affection for the parent. Indeed, sometimes it goes further than that, making the child hope that the parent will die. There's nothing which can excuse that thought in a child, but it is very wrong for the parent to put the temptation the child's way.

In the second place it starts the child trying to supply his needs in dishonest ways. And once people have started along this road, perhaps because of the meanness of their parents, they tend to stay on it even though the reason for starting vanishes. So parents ought to be very careful not to put their children in danger. Besides, the parent loses the delight of seeing his children live prosperously and comfortably; only a crawling insect would exchange that joy for the so-called pleasure of having vast sums in the bank.

If a parent intends to give money to his children, he must take care that he has come by it honestly. There is a curse that rests on money or property that has been come by dishonestly. If you leave a legacy like that to your child you cheat and deceive him. The wealth you pass on is make-believe, like a rotten apple, and the decay will eventually eat it all away. That's no way of providing for a child!

It is better to have a little, honestly earned, than to have a large income gathered dishonestly. (Proverbs 16.8)

Setting an example to children

Parents must set their children a good example; that's not only giving them rules about being good, but being a living pattern that they can copy. The influence of example is far more telling than that of rules – especially where there is a great respect for the person giving the example, and when there's plenty of opportunity to talk about why we should do some things and not others. Both respect and confidences are present in a good parent-child relationship.

How careful a parent must be to behave properly in front of his children! For the parent's example is a way of winning them to good living. We are in a desperate situation at the moment; if men and women allow themselves freedom to do all sorts of evil, it is inevitable that children seeing this will imitate it. If a child sees his father drunk, he will surely think that it's all right for him to get drunk as well. If he hears him swear he will do the same...and so on for all the other vices. Then, if the parent is more concerned about his child's behaviour than his own and forbids the child the things which he himself does, or punishes the child for doing them, it's certain that the child will think it most unfair: 'My father is punishing me for a thing which he frequently does himself.' So the child is hardly likely to be impressed by what his father tells him is right. Parents must therefore live a Christian life. If they do not, they put at risk not only their own souls but those of their children and, as it were, leave to them an inheritance in hell.

Parent must pray for their children every day. With great energy they must commend them to God's care and blessings which come to them will pass on to future generations. The Bible often talks about the blessing which goes on from one generation to another. The great example was the Jewish nation; though they were so disobedient and provoked God, yet the godliness of their parents – their ancestors Abraham, Isaac and Jacob – moved God to save them from destruction. On the other hand, even good men have fared badly because of the wrong that their parents did. So if parents have any real love for their children, any genuine desire for their prosperity, let them be very careful to bring blessings on them by living godly lives themselves.

Finally, parents must take care that they use their position of authority over their children with truth and care. They must not oppress them with unreasonable orders simply to prove their own authority.

When children come to marriage

In every important matter they must consider the lasting good of their children and not make them do anything which is inconsistent with this aim. Nothing is more important in this respect than the future marriage of their children. Many who in other respects have been good parents are somewhat to blame here. Keen to get them married to a prosperous family they persuade them against their own inclination. This is tyranny. It leads to a great deal of trouble which all the wealth in the world cannot repair.

Two things above all parents should look for in introducing their children to the right young people. In the first place they need to be sure that their child can live out a Christian life; so they should encourage friendship with a good Christian. The second consideration is that their children may live happily and comfortably in this world. So it's important to look for companions who really can provide for them, remembering all the time that wealth is not a prerequisite for a satisfactory marriage, and that parents should not be over-persuasive.

What is far more important is that the pair are kind to each other and deeply love each other. Without that, marriage is a most uncomfortable state of affairs and no parent ought to push a child into it.

RELATIVES

The duty of natural (as against our spiritual) brothers and sisters is to be united in affection and concern. Except that they are of the same physical make-up so they ought to have all the more mutual kindness and understanding. Abraham says to his cousin Lot that they should not be quarrelling because, 'We are relatives' (Genesis 13.8). So, to some degree, we owe this sort of kindness to any who are are blood relations.

This duty of love must be very firmly rooted in the hearts of brothers and sisters. If it isn't, they are in more danger of disagreeing than anyone else. For as long as they live together in their parents' home they have ample opportunity to fall out. Again, because they are in a sense equals – as being born of the same parents – they are in a position to be envious of each other, especially when one gets something the other doesn't. You remember that Joseph's brothers envied him because his father took more notice of him than he did of the others. Rachel was jealous of her sister Leah who had children. So, all of you who have brothers and sisters must take care be to genuinely loving and kind to them in order to avoid becoming jealous. Think of them as part of yourselves, and then you will never consider it right to quarrel with them, or be jealous of any advantage they may have – any more than you would imagine one part of your body could be jealous of another. Each strives to advantage and help the other.

BELIEVERS

Then there's a spiritual tie between us and those who profess the same Christian faith as ourselves. We ought to honour the relationship we have to each other. We owe to our brothers and sisters in Christ a great deal of tenderness and affection. Of all ties, the spiritual one should be most close to our hearts.

Respect everyone, love your fellow believers. (1 Peter 2.17)

So then, as often as we have the chance, we should do good to everyone, and especially to those who belong to our family in the faith. (Galatians 6.10)

We are to be most loving and kind to our brothers and sisters in the faith. Jesus says

You can be sure that whoever gives even a drink of cold water to one of the least of these my followers because he is my follower, will certainly receive a reward. (Matthew 10.42)

From this we can know that Christ wants us to care for other Christians.

Our fellowship with our brothers and sisters in Christ must be one of shared doctrine – 'the faith which once and for all God has given to his people' (Jude 3). We must keep this unity whatever storms of opposition blow around us:

> Let us hold on firmly to the hope we profess, because we can trust God to keep his promise. Let us be concerned for one another, to help one another to show love and to do good. Let us not give up the habit of meeting together, as some are doing. Instead let us encourage one another all the more, since you see that the Day of the Lord is coming nearer. (Hebrews 10.23-25)

We are to be united with our fellow Christians in worship too. We must be regularly amongst a congregation of Christian people, for this is the outward sign of our inner conviction of faith. So if someone withdraws from fellowship, we might well suspect that he is giving up his faith. The first Christians were very loyal in this way:

> They devoted themselves to the Apostles' teaching and to the fellowship, to the breaking of bread and to prayer. (Acts 2.42)

They 'devoted themselves' – they were not put off by opposition even though it was quite acute in the early days. We learn from this that we are still obliged to meet together even if that meeting becomes dangerous.

Then, we are to put up with the weaknesses of our Christian brothers and sisters and to support them. St Paul says,

> We who are strong in the faith ought to help the weak to carry their burdens. (Romans 15.1)

We are not to despise a Christian brother or sister, or refuse to have fellowship with him if he is in error at some point as long as he is holding on to all the essentials of the Christian faith. St Paul instances the case of a new and immature Christian who had needless scruples about what he should and should not eat (Romans chapter 14). More experienced Christians who had deeper understanding of the faith saw that error. But Paul tells them to welcome him any way, and not to despise him. At the same time he tells the Christian not to judge his stronger brothers and sisters. Whatever our differences of opinion, they must be tolerated on both sides, and they must not in the slightest diminish our family love for each other.

> My brothers, if someone is caught in any kind of wrong-doing, those of you who are spiritual should set him right. But you must do it in a gentle way. And keep an eye on yourselves, so that you will not be tempted too. Help to carry one another's burdens, and in this way you will obey the law of Christ. (Galatians 6.1-2)

If our brothers and sisters in Christ fall, we are not to look on them as failures. Nor are we to be proud of our own standing like the Pharisee in Jesus' parable (Luke 18.11). We have a responsibility to help our fellow Christians to recover. And we need to remember that we are not so strong as to be immune from failure ourselves.

Sympathy and a caring love is required from us. We must take to heart the predicaments of our brothers and sisters as individuals or as members of society. They are part of the church, that is the 'Church Universal', the fellowship of all believing people throughout the world; or part of a national church, that is all the believers in a nation. Whatever happens to either of these communities – the whole church in general or any one part of it – must concern us, especially if it is that part of the church in which we ourselves are members. We can rejoice at its progress and feel its shortcomings. The Paslmist expresses this empathy in Psalm 51:

> Oh God, be kind to Zion and help her; rebuild the walls of Jersualem. (Psalm 51.18)

Anybody who remains unaffected by the condition of the church cannot be thought of as a living member of it. If there are persecutions and set-backs anywhere in the church, we must be especially concerned:

> Oh Lord, the time has come to have mercy on Zion; this is the right time. Your servants love her even though she is destroyed. They have pity on her even though she is in ruins. (Psalm 102.13,14)

In the same way we are to have this family feeling towards our brothers and sisters as individuals. We have to take an interest in every Christian person; to share with each in joy and sorrow.

> Be happy with those who are happy, weep with those who weep; have the same concern for everyone. (Romans 12.15,16)

If one part of the body suffers, all the other parts suffer with it; if one part is praised, all the other parts share its happiness. (1 Corinthians 12.26)

Such is the kind of love that we must show to our brothers and sisters in Christ; Christ himself has made it the mark of his followers:

And now I give you a new commandment: Love one another. As I have loved you, so you must love one another. If you have love for one another, then everyone will know that you are my disciples. (John 13.34,35)

So we cannot both be Christ's disciples and unloving towards members of the Christian family.

HUSBANDS, WIVES

The relationship between husband and wife is closer than those we have spoken of so far.

A man will leave his father and mother and be united to his wife and the two will become one flesh. (Ephesians 5.31)

The husband and the wife each have duties towards the other. The wife owes submissiveness:

Wives, submit to your husbands, as is fitting in the Lord. (Colossians 3.18)

Note the words 'As is fitting in the Lord'. There is no suggestion that the wife must do anything of which God does not approve. For God is above man. A wife must not do something that her husband tells her to do which is forbidden by God.

But let us suppose that the husband asks the wife to do not something which is against God's law, but something which is unhelpful and unwise? Well, of course, it's not contrary to our rule of submissiveness for the wife calmly and gently to point out the inappropriateness of what is being asked, and to persuade her husband to change his mind. But sharp language is not to be used, and in the long run it would be right for the wife to do what the husband is asking if it is not against the law of God.

The wife has the duty of faithfulness towards her husband. She must be faithful in intimate relationship with him, not letting anyone else make love to her. She musn't listen to any other man who wants to make advances, but reject the suggestion with abhorrence, and make sure that he doesn't get the chance to try again.

Secondly there's to be faithfulness in terms of her management of home and property. She must think of her husband's interests and never deceive him. She should not misappropriate what he gives her.

The wife owes her husband love and affection in her manner and behaviour:

> The Lord God said, 'It is not good for the man to be alone. I will make him a helper suitable for him'. (Genesis 2.18)

She must bring him as much help as possible and make his life as untroubled as possible. This principle applies in health or illness, poverty or wealth. So moodiness and bitter words, argument and restiveness are all to be shunned. They would bring on the husband heaviness and anxiety instead of health and comfort. Besides, if it's wrong to behave like this with anyone else (and we have seen that already), how much worse must it be to behave hurtfully to one who should be receiving the greatest kindness and love from us?

The fact that a husband is difficult or inadequate in some way does not justify the wife shaking herself free from her obligations. When God tells us what we're to do for somebody, it doesn't excuse us from doing it if the person is unworthy. In fact, in these circumstances it becomes all the more imperative for a wife to behave gently and kindly, in order to convict him and bring a change of heart.

> You wives must submit to your husbands, so that if any of them do not believe God's word, your conduct will win them over to believe. It will not be necessary for you to say a word, because they will see how pure and reverent your conduct is. (1 Peter 3.1-2)

As we read history, it becomes apparent that the behaviour of Christian wives has been a powerful instrument in winning men to faith. If only women still had the patience to try, it might have the same effect again. At the very least there would be more peace among families. There must be many homes where things work in quite the opposite way, and men have fallen into bad company, drinking and poverty, simply to get away from domestic quarrels. Let every wife beware of putting this sort of temptation in front of her husband. And when he does anything which out of kindness she ought to scold him for, let it be gently and mildly, so that it is obvious to him that she speaks from love and not from anger.

The husband, too, has his responsibilities. The first is love, which St Paul insists must be deep and understanding towards his wife. We learn this by the picture of Christ's love for the church painted in Ephesians:

> Husbands, love your wives just as Christ loved the church and have his life for it. (Ephesians 5.25)

And he adds,

> No one ever hates his own body. Instead he feeds it and takes care of it, just as Christ does the church; for we are members of his body. (Ephesians 5.29)

If husbands realise that their love must be Christ-like, they will understand that they can never treat their wives rudely or brutally. If they think of them as part of themselves, they will not hurt them any more than they would their own bodies. Let those husbands who tyrannise their wives stop to think if that's the way they would love their own bodies!

The husband has the duty of faithfulness to the intimacies of marriage. He is to make love only to his wife. This faithfulness is required by God of the husband just as much as of the wife. And though people in general seem to look less severely upon the *man* when he commits adultery, God makes no difference in this respect between man and woman. It is also a breach of the marriage vow; as well as being sinful in itself it is therefore the breaking of a promise to God.

The husband is also responsible for providing for the wife in every way he should. He must let her share everything that God has blessed him with. He musn't be mean and prevent her from enjoying what is her right, nor must he be spendthrift and waste his money so that there is nothing for her to have. The husband, as we have seen, must consider his wife part of his own body, and so he must look after her in exactly the same way as he looks after himself. That is no excuse for the wife not to contribute her work towards the well-being of the family; it's just as wrong if the husband has to work hard while the wife sits doing nothing.

The husband has the responsibility for making the wife conscious of Christian truth if she herself has little grasp of it. This is the implication of 1 Corinthians 14.35. In fact the husband has the responsibility of making sure that his whole family has Christian teaching. This should make men more careful to gain knowledge themselves so that they can carry out their duty properly.

Husbands and wives, pray for each other! Pray about health, and pray about faith as well. Being good to each other includes Christian good. Back him up when he wants to do the right thing.

Stop her when she's obviously wrong. Work it out together.

What about your family? Can you both help them in any way? And your neighbours and friends? Is there anything they need? Get each other going at being kind, and doing the right thing. This is what love is all about.

These couples who don't care if each other gets into bad ways – you can't tell me they're in love! If only husbands and wives would really give themselves to Christ, their marriages would be heaven. It would cut out rows for a start. Rows are a family disease and can be sheer hell. Let's face it, if marriage isn't built on Christian love, it's not worth getting into.

Everyone who intends to get married should think carefully first, and choose someone with whom they can have spiritual kinship; in other words someone who genuinely reveres God. There are many wrong reasons for marriage about today. Some marry for money, others for good looks. More often than not it is these wordly aspects alone that people consider. But whoever wants Christian marriage should look to making his marriage useful in the better cause of serving God and saving his own soul. At least he must be sure that it is no obstacle to these things. So the character of the partner whom he or she chooses is more important than all the money in the world; though I do recognise that one should think economically as well!

More important, don't enter into a marriage which is not only potentially harmful, but is also sinful in itself. For instance, getting married to someone who is already committed. He or she rightly belongs to the party to whom the former promise was made. For another to marry them during the life-time of their previous marriage partner is to take the husband or wife away from that partner – that would be adultery:

A married woman, for example, is bound by the law to her husband as long as he lives; but if he dies, then she is free from the law that bound her to him. So then, if she lives with another man while her husband is alive she will be called an adulteress; but if her husband dies, she is legally a free woman and does not commit adultery if she marries another man. (Romans 7.2-3)

Chapters 18 and 20 of the book Leviticus list those relations whom it is wrong for us to marry. Whoever marries close to himself or to his deceased wife commits the sin of incest, and he remains guilty as long as he continues to live with her. If people were only more careful before they made decisions to marry, society would avoid many of the unfortunate affects which we see around us. For the advantage of everyone, people should look on marriage as our church advises:

It is a way of life that all should honour; and it must not be undertaken carelessly, lightly, or selfishly, but reverently, responsibly, and after serious thought. *(The marriage service of the Church of England)*

If we follow this advice God will bless us. If we don't follow it, there is little hope of blessing.

FRIENDS

If friendship is on the right foundations it is of great help and advantage. But there is no relationship more genuinely misunderstood. People use the term 'friends' for those whom they see often and so share a certain proximity with – even if that means no more than a mutual agreement to do something wrong! The drunkard will call anyone a friend who drinks with him. The confidence trickster will call his partner a 'friend'. If you are proud you will think of your flatterers as 'friends'. And so it is with all things wrong; those who help us in them we call our 'friends'. But in God's eyes this is far from friendship. The devil himself can make us a very good 'friend' when we need him for these purposes. True friendship is quite the opposite. It happens when someone encourages us to do good, not to do evil. A true friend loves us sufficiently to be concerned for our good, and will never be the cause of bringing us down.

Here is an analysis of friendship:

1. Friendship keeps promises and confidences. Everyone is disgusted by a friend who betrays his trust. 'Even if you have a violent argument with a friend, and speak sharply, all is not lost. You can still make it up with him. But any friend will leave you if you insult him, if you are arrogant, if you reveal his secrets, or if you turn on him unexpectedly' (Ecclesiasticus 22.22).

2. Friendship is help and advice where it is needed; it is encouragement and comfort; it is generosity in need; it is rescue in trouble and danger. If you want to read a Bible illustration of friendship examine 1 Samuel, chapter 20 – the friendship of Jonathan and David: 'Jonathan loved David as much as he loved himself' (1 Samuel 20.17).

3. Friendship is spiritual help and guidance. It involves encouraging your friend to do good and dissuading him or her from doing evil. Friends alone can speak to each other of their faults; so theirs is a special responsibility. If you don't help your friend to see faults, then you let him down badly because he will be confident that there is nothing wrong. Everyone has need of being advised in this way at some time or other so it is heartless to neglect to help and advise. We naturally give ourselves the benefit of the doubt, so we cannot see our own faults as clearly as we see the faults of others. Somebody has to show us, and as soon as possible stop things gettng worse. If faults continue unchecked they turn into habits and then it's too late for correction. Before God we have a duty not to be silent when we should be showing our friendship in this way. It is just as well for anyone who has entered into an accepted friendship to come to an agreement: that each will warn and correct the other. So it becomes part of the friendship to offer advice, and can never be mistaken by either for interference or unkind criticism.

4. Friendship involves praying. Not only should we help our friends directly, but we should ask God to help them too; praying that he will bless them in body and soul.

5. Finally friendship is faithfulness; not playing fast and loose with our friend. We shouldn't carelessly grow weary of friends because we have had them a long time. That is a great injustice to them. The longer they have been good friends to us, the higher we should hold them in our esteem. A casual attitute towards friends is stupid from our own point of view, for it's throwing away the greatest treasure of human experience:

> Do not forget your friends or your father's friends. (Proverbs 27.10)

More than this, do not take offence at any small thing that a friend might do which you dislike. You must make allowance for human weakness. If you forgive your friend today, you offer him the chance to make up for it tomorrow. Nothing but a friend's persistent unfaithfulness or remorseless wickedness should give you cause to break this bond.

EMPLOYEES

The duty of the employee is to carry out all proper directions the

employer gives him. The pattern for this is set down by St Paul in
Ephesians:

> Obey your human masters with fear and trembling; and do it
> with a sincere heart, as though you were serving Christ. Do this
> not only when they are watching you, because you want to gain
> their approval, but with all your heart do what God wants, as
> servants of Christ. Do your work cheerfully as though you served
> the Lord, and not merely men. Remember that the Lord will
> reward everyone...for the good work he does. (Ephesians 6.5-8)

So it is that the employee must not be grumbling and unwilling,
but alert and cheerful, remembering that he is responsible to God
for his attitude, and not to men. And Paul reminds us to be
conscious of God's reward.

Employees must be honest; this means doing things thoroughly,
and not only when the employer is watching. They must also be
faithful and reliable when they are trusted to do something. St Paul
sets out this principle in his letter to Titus:

> Slaves are to submit to their masters and please them in all
> things. They must not anwer them back or steal from them.
> Instead they must show that they are always good and faithful,
> so as to bring credit to the teaching about God our Saviour in all
> they do. (Titus 2.9-10)

Misappropriation of funds or goods with which employees have
been trusted is no better than stealing. And this principle applies
just as much to other ways of hurting an employer; taking bribes to
make damaging contracts etc. In fact this sort of dishonesty is
worse than stealing, because it involves a greater betrayal of trust
and so adds to the crime. The same applies to wasting the
employer's money and materials. It's just as bad for a company if it
loses through an employee's negligence as by his greed. The breach
of trust is the same. For every employer entrusts his affairs to his
employees' care, as well as to their honesty. It's no good the
employer being sure that his servants won't cheat him, if by sheer
negligence they let someone elso do it!

By the examples St Paul gives, employees should act civilly and
respectfully towards their masters, not answering them back, nor
being rude or unpleasant to them. In fact St Peter argues that even
when we are corrected for something we haven't done, we should
be prepared to suffer for it:

If you endure suffering even when you have done right, God will
bless you for it. (1 Peter 2.20)

What's more, if he has to be corrected, the employee must not only
listen carefully to the employer's criticism, but never be satisfied
until he has put the fault right. Finally the employee must take
constant care during working hours; there is not to be laziness or
going slow, nor playing games or fooling about with other people.
For it's not only the employer's anger that the employee should be
avoiding but God's. God will call each of us to account and we will
have to answer for how we have behaved towards those who are set
over us in this world.

EMPLOYERS

On the other side, the employer also has his responsibilities. He is
to be just, and must satisfy the conditions on which his staff were
taken on; conditions as in respect of pay food, etc. Any employer
who withholds his employee's rights is an oppressor.

The employer has a responsibility to correct in his staff where
there are faults. I'm not talking just about faults in their work – few
employers are slow at doing that! I mean faults against God, which
should trouble him more than his own loss or inconvenience. God's
dishonour and the danger to his employees' soul should worry him
far more than bad workmanship. So when you see employers
irritated by some trivial negligence yet unperturbed about sins
against God, it is a sign that they have become too selfish and
neither God's glory nor their employees' souls matter to them.
Such an attitude is all too common amongst employers. On the
whole they couldn't care less how their employees behave towards
God, and the problems and profanities of their employees' families
don't worry them either. They never stop to warn or encourage
them or help them from falling into trouble. Such employers forget
that they will have to give an account to God one day.

It is the duty of every person in charge to try to advance respect
for God among all those who are under him. That applies just as
much to the leader of a family as to the leader of the nation. Psalm
101 sets out this principle, and it affects everyone from the top of
society to the bottom. If employers applied this principle not only
would they benefit by God's rewards, but their businesses would
thrive too. For in so far as employees have consciences enlightened
by God, they will never dream of being negligent or dishonest.

When an employer disciplines or corrects his staff he must do it in such a manner as will make them most likely to improve. In other words, losing your temper just won't work. The employee will end up despising and hating his employer. The employer's intervention must be moderate in order to convince the employee of the mistake and, at the same time, give him confidence that the correcting is done out of a desire to put things right and not to vent the employer's bad temper.

The employer himself must set an honest and Christian example to his staff. If he doesn't, no amount of encouragement or correction from him will ever do any good. An employer's bad example will pull down far more than he can build up with wise words. For instance, it's quite useless for a drunken or blasphemous employer to expect a responsible and principled staff.

The employer is to make provision for his employees to be instructed in their duties towards God. He must allow them time for public worship, and to practise their faith amongst their own family.

The employer must not lay greater burdens on his employees than they are able to bear; his orders must be reasonable and moderate. His requirements of work from them must be balanced; enabling them to have enough time to take seriously their responsibilities towards God, and yet making sure they don't get into lazy habits. That would make them useless to him and open to malpractices.

Finally he is to encourage them when they do well. He must meet their reliability, care and Christian behaviour with the generosity and kindness which it deserves. And in all his dealings with them he must remember that he himself is responsible to the 'Master in heaven' (Ephesians 6.9).

LOVE

Jesus said, 'I give you a new commandment; love one another. As I have loved you, so you must love one another. If you have love for one another, then everyone will know that you are my disciples.' (John 13.34,35)

My commandment is this: love one another, just as I love you. This, then, is what I command you: love one another. (John 15.12,17)

You can see by St John's Gospel's repeated reference to loving one another, and by the fact that the whole of the letter 1 John is an encouragement to love, that loving one another is a matter of the first importance for Christians. In fact, Jesus says that is how they will be recognised,

> If you have love for one another, then everyone will know that you are my disciples. (John 13.35)

Love shows itself in feeling and actions. If we really love someone we'll be kind to them in every way – kind to their souls, their bodies, their goods, their possessions, and their reputation.

If only we had the least spark of true love in us we would desire good for people's souls – those precious things Christ bought with his own blood; the souls he loved so tenderly. If we don't love one another this much, we are far from obeying the command to love as he has loved. His love for souls shows itself in two ways – he wants to purify them here by his grace and to make them happy forever in his glory. This is the way we are to be kind, copying his example; wanting people to achieve purity and holiness here which will enable them to be eternally happy in heaven. Why should we be frightened of being damned ourselves, yet not care about other people?

Physically, too, we are to be concerned for the good of others. We take enough care of ourselves, anxious to avoid the least pain or illness. Love extends this care and tenderness to other people. Whatever worries us we should be unwilling to let happen to another. The same applies to property and to reputation. We ourselves like to live comfortably, so we should be concerned that others do, or we shall not 'love our neighbour as we love ourselves'.

If we feel love for others it will stop us from deliberately upsetting them. We will try to keep the peace and hold our temper. We will not be 'ill-mannered or selfish or irritable'. (1 Corinthians 13.5) We will be sympathetic to others in their trouble, taking others' misfortune as our own – crying when they cry. We shall be happy when they are fortunate. St Paul tells us,

> Be happy with those who are happy, weep with those who weep. (Roman 12.15)

Our love for others will encourage us to pray for them. We are ourselves powerless to bring them the blessings we want for them, so we must approach God on their behalf:

> Every good gift and every perfect present comes from heaven; it comes down from God. (James 2.17)

What is kindness to our neighbour without prayer for him? Not worth considering – a kind of empty compliment. Can anyone really believe that you wish them well if you won't put vigour and effectiveness into your well-wishing – by praying? Wishes without prayer are unhelpful and fruitless. St Paul says,

> I urge that petitions, prayers, requests, and thanksgivings be offered to God for all people. (1 Timothy 2.1)

Praying comes so naturally from loving, that anyone who thinks he loves someone but can't bring himself to pray is simply deceiving himself.

Love is not jealous. (1 Corinthians 13.4)

Love guards the mind from jealousy. Common sense should tell us that we can't love someone and be jealous of them at the same time; for to be jealous is to be unhappy at their good fortune. But love desires their good fortune. So if we are possessed by love for someone, that love will certainly squeeze out any jealousy.

Love is not conceited or proud. (1 Corinthians 13.4)

Love and humility are linked together in the New Testament. Where we are commanded to love, we are commanded to be humble too:

> You are the people of God; he loved you and chose you for his own. So then, you must clothe yourselves with compassion, kindness, humility, gentleness and patience. (Colossians 3.12)

> Love one another warmly as Christian brothers, and be eager to show respect for one another. (Romans 12.10)

See how humility keeps company with love – in fact, it flows from it. For love sets a price and value upon the thing loved, and makes us prize it.

Loving ourselves makes us think highly of ourselves. If we turn this love outward and love our brothers and sisters, that love will equally cetainly make us humble, so that we can think highly of them. We shall see those characteristics and qualities of theirs which we overlook when we are being proud.

Love does not keep a record of wrongs; love never gives up; and its faith, hope and patience never fail. (1 Corinthians 13.5,7)

On the one hand love will not entertain gossip about other people;

on the other it is willing to give them the benefit of the doubt, believing and hoping the best. Experience tells us this, because when we are in love with someone we often can't see his faults. However large they are, we are blind to them. So, love will scarcely create faults in the beloved, or magnify them beyond their real size. Which just goes to show how unloving it is to think evil of other people without cause.

Love must be completely sincere. (Romans 12.9)

Love rules out all counterfeit emotions. You can't imitate love. Real love and poor copies are as far apart as the natural world and drawings of it. False love is hypocrisy and much to be feared. All too often we see people profess that they love others, but as soon as their backs are turned they make mischief for them or harshly criticise them.

Love is not rude, it is not self seeking, it is not easily angered. (1 Corinthians 13.5)

Love has a generous and noble disposition, it doesn't think in terms of profits or personal advantage. So anything which masquerades as love but is really selfishness is very far away from the truth.

LOVE AND FORGIVENESS

Love turns out of the heart all ill will and any desire for revenge. It is impossible that both love and such things should survive together in the same individual. Love can endure the greatest injury without a thought of paying it back. Love's only response is to pray for blessing on the person who has done the injury. So it is that a malicious and revengeful person has nothing of love about him.

Love cannot be exclusive. A man can claim to love one person deeply yet hate another bitterly. Christian love cannot be restricted like this; it must extend to everybody in the world – not least to our enemies. If it doesn't, it is not the divine love taught by Christ:

Why should God reward you if you love only the people who love you? Even the tax collectors do that! (Matthew 5.46)

Jesus wants better things from his followers, and so has given us the instruction to love even our enemies:

You have heard that it was said, 'Love your friends, hate your

enemies.' But now I tell you: love your enemies and pray for
those who persecute you, so that you may become the sons of
your Father in heaven. (Matthew 5.34,44)

If you don't love like this he will not recognise you as one of his
followers. So, you see, all we have said about love applies to our
most spiteful enemy just as much as to our most considerate friend.
Humanly speaking there might be good reason to object, so let's
spend a little time considering why we should love our enemies.

First, think how much there is about loving – and forgiving – in
the New Testament:

Be kind and tender-hearted to one another, and forgive one
another as God has forgiven you through Christ. (Ephesians 4.32)

Be tolerant with one another and forgive one another whenever
any of you has a complaint against someone else. You must forgive
one another just as the Lord has forgiven you. (Colossians 3.13)

Do not pay back evil with evil or cursing with cursing; instead,
pay back with a blessing, because a blessing is what God
promised to give you when he called you. (1 Peter 3.9)

There are plenty more texts we could use to make the point, but
these should be enough to convince anyone that love with forgiveness is part of Christian behaviour.

I would think that there are few who have heard the gospel who
would doubt this. That is why it is so very odd that many who call
themselves Christians should give no heed to the command what-
soever. People will say publicly and often that they will not forgive
so-and-so. Telling them what Christ has commanded doesn't
change their attitude. Such people surely can't understand what is
meant by the word 'Christian'. It means a servant, a disciple and
follower of Christ. Love is the mark of the servant, and the
continual study of the follower. So it is quite absurd that people
should say they are Christians and at the same time resist the
express wishes of Christ whom they say is their master.

Why do you call me, 'Lord, Lord,' and yet don't do what I tell
you? (Luke 6.46)

If you think of the whole world as divided into two great families,
Christ's family and Satan's family, then you can see which family
anyone belongs to by the amount of notice they take of the head of
the family; if they obey Christ, they are Christ's, if they obey Satan

they are Satan's. Revenge and retaliation is so much part of the devil's regime that there is no better way of obeying him – wearing his colours and proclaiming which family we belong to – than by being unloving and unforgiving. So it's quite ridiculous and impudent for you to suggest that you are Christ's servant if you intend to do the devil's work. You had better count on Christ disowning you and handing you back to your proper employer to get your wages in hell.

Love your enemies and do good to them; lend and expect nothing back. You will then have a great reward, and you will be sons of the most high God. For he is good to the ungrateful and the wicked. Be merciful just as your Father is merciful. (Luke 7.35,36)

Jesus points to God as an example of love. He tells us that loving our enemies will make us 'sons of the Most High God' – it will give us the resemblance to him that children have to their parents. God is kind to the ungrateful and to the wicked.

He makes his sun to shine on bad and good people alike, and gives rain to those who do good and to those who do evil. (Matthew 5.45)

God is the source of all perfection. Being like him is the greatest thing we could wish for; imitating him – our Father – is the special mark of his child. God's kindness and goodness to his enemies is apparent not only in the world around us but also in his spiritual mercy. In some sense we have all been his enemies:

At one time you were far away from God and were his enemies because of the evil things you did and thought. (Colossians 1.21)

And the penalty of that enmity with God would have fallen on our own heads. Yet God desired reconciliation with us from no other motive except his great mercy. Far from having any thought of revenge, he made plans to bring us back to himself and give us peace. In itself this was massive love and kindness, but the means God used went even beyond that. He sent his own Son from heaven to effect his plan – not just to persuade us, but to suffer for us too. So much did he value us pitiful creatures that he didn't think the blood of his Son was to high a price to pay. Jesus laid down his life for us his enemies:

Christ himself carried our sins in his body to the cross, so that we might die to sin and live for righteousness. It is by his wounds that you have been healed. (1 Peter 2.24)

When the truth of this comes home to us we can only draw St John's conclusion,

> Dear friends, if God loved us this much, then surely we should love one another. (1 John 4.11)

How wrong it is for us to harbour grievances against our brothers and sisters when God puts his aside – and that when we have provoked him so much!

Let's compare for a moment our offences against God with other people's offences against us. What a difference there is! When we offend God we are offending against the Sovereign Power of the universe, to whom we owe obedience. We are showing wicked ingratitude to one who has been so generous to us. Others couldn't possibly offend us so greatly. However kind we might have been towards them, it could not be as kind as God has been to us. Then, think how often our sins against God are far in excess of anything anybody does to us. Jesus sets out the ratio of what others owe us and what we owe God in the parable of Matthew 18. Their debt is in tens, but our debt to God is in millions! God forgives us so much more than we could ever need to forgive our brothers and sisters.

We have said as much as we can to silence the criticism of cruel and revengeful people who think it is right to retaliate. Worse, they think it is quite unreasonable and stupid that Christians refuse to retaliate. Yet God himself loves his enemies – to a much higher degree then ever we can. Who dares say that it is irrational to love enemies? To say that God acts stupidly is blasphemy. If any spiritual duty like this appears foolish, then St Paul tells us why:

> Whoever does not have the Spirit cannot receive the gifts that come from God's Spirit. Such a person really does not under-stand them. They are nonsense to him, because their value can be judged only on a spiritual basis. (1 Corinthians 2.14)

It is the wordliness of our own thinking that makes God's ways seem foolish. So, instead of protesting against our obligations, let's clean up our hearts and minds and we shall find the truth of the proverb:

> To the man with insight, it is all clear: to the well-informed, it is all plain. (Proverbs 8.9)

Loving your enemies is not only a logical thing to do, it's a pleasant duty. Nobody can really know this unless they've tried it. It's the same with every human pleasure; you have to taste it first before you can tell another how delicious it is. And what is true of human pleasures is all the more true of spiritual. If you really want to know the joy of loving your enemies, try it and then you will be convinced. In the meantime don't be prejudiced.

Although I'm suggesting a practical proof, you should be able to guess at the results even before you start – simply by comparing the practice of loving your enemies with its alternative. Hatred and revenge are restless and tormenting emotions, and they quite take over people's minds, consuming their time and disturbing their sleep:

> Wicked people cannot sleep unless they have done something wrong. They lie awake unless they have hurt someone. (Proverbs 4.16)

A good example of this in the Old Testament is Haman (in Esther chapter 5), who couldn't enjoy anything because he hated Mordecai so much.

On the other hand the peaceable person who takes no notice of hurts and insults enjoys a continual calmness. Let his enemies do what they may, they can't rob him of his peace; he's like a rock which no storm or wind can move. The bitter and revengeful man is more like a wave of the sea which the wind whips up. And not only is there a commotion going on inside him, but everything goes wrong outside as well. He makes his enemies furious by retaliating, and provokes them to do them even more harm. Sometimes vengeful people shipwreck themselves in pursuit of their revenge; it's quite common to see people sacrificing property, peace, public standing – even their life and soul – not caring how much it hurts them, because they want to be spiteful towards their enemies! Temper has blinded them! On the other hand, the quiet and peaceable person melts his opponent and placates anger.

> A gentle answer quietens anger, but a harsh one stirs it up. (Proverbs 16.1)

Even if his peaceable nature didn't make any impression, he would still gain the opportunity of showing Christian love and forgiveness; obeying Christ's command and copying his example. There is a reward for this to be gained in heaven. If someone objects that we shouldn't take rewards into consideration, let me say that it is quite proper to expect a reward – something which we will enjoy far more than any temporal pleasure.

Consider, too, the danger of not loving our enemies; we could forfeit our own pardon from God – the devil would like this very much.

Just think about that, and then tell me what you have gained by the most successful revenge that you have ever perpetrated. People say 'revenge is sweet', but is there any sweetness that can make up for the eternal bitterness that revenge brings on us? The trouble is that we just don't stop to think this out, but get hurried along by our hot tempers. This is the way of the drowsy bee that stings someone and leaves the sting behind, so killing itself at the same time. The bee might have caused some pain for a short time, but any onlooker would admit that – of the two – the bee has come off worse. It's just the same with us; we might sting others for a short time – put them to some temporary trouble – but compared with what will happen to us, it's nothing; the sorrow we bring on ourselves is eternal. So remember, when you are shooting at an enemy, you're going to miss and hit yourself. Let nobody temporise with himself and think that these fears are in vain. Don't let him think that he's going to be forgiven by God if he won't forgive the one on whom he is taking revenge. Jesus, who speaks truly, has told us quite the opposite:

If you do not forgive others, then your Father will not forgive the wrongs you have done. (Matthew 6.15)

Jesus' parable of the servant in Matthew 18 sets this out in greater detail. The servant had been forgiven a great debt by his master and yet was so cruel to his fellow-servant as to persecute him for a few coins. What happens? The master cancels his earlier forgiveness and once again insists that the servant pay the whole debt. Jesus applies this to us.

That is how my Father in heaven will treat every one of you unless you forgive your brother from your heart. (Matthew 18.35)

Finally let me speak of gratitude. God has been wonderfully kind to us; Christ has suffered so much to bring us within the mercy and forgiveness of God. Haven't we some obligation to return that love? Paul tells us,

We are ruled by the love of Christ...he died for all so that those who live should no longer live for themselves, but only for him who died and was raised to life for their sake. (2 Corinthians 5.15)

How thankless we are if we deny God such a little thing as this – to forgive other people!

The peace and unity of Christians was something very much prized and valued by Jesus. When he was to go from the world he considered it the most precious thing he could leave behind:

> Peace is what I leave with you; it is my own peace that I give you. (John 14.27)

We are accustomed to setting great store by the smallest wishes of our departed friends, and taking great care to do them. So it's obvious that we don't really love Christ if we treat his wishes with any less deference.

Just one more work of advice: rememver to stop yourself in time. Draw back from the first inclination to be bitter. It's much better that the teaching we have just considered should act as an armour against the onslaught of feelings of revenge, than it should have to be a disinfectant to clean the wound afterwards. If you have some feelings of bitterness even at this moment, don't hesitate. Don't let them go round and round in your mind. Be a good student of Christ. Take the chance of obeying and pleasing God; take it now before the spark turns to flames. Choose life rather than death!

LOVE IN ACTION

> Do you need evidence that faith without actions is useless? (James 2.20)

> Our love should not be just words and talk; it must be true love, which shows itself in action. (1 John 3.18)

Every soul has both its physical and spiritual aspects. Real love requires us to do good to people in both senses. In so far as their soul includes their minds, we must try to comfort and refresh those who are our brothers and sisters. We must want to give them reason to be happy and cheerful. When we see that they are sad or depressed we should apply such medicine as we have as Christians – working to lift their depression. St Paul reminds us:

> God helps us in all our troubles, so that we are able to help others who have all kinds of trouble using the same help that we ourselves have received from God. (1 Corinthians 1.4)

But the soul in the *spiritual* sense is of even greater concern. To be of help here is much more important than cheering up the mind alone. For the deepest sorrows of this life are vastly exceeded by the eternal sorrows and the sadnesses of hell. And so, though we must not leave out care for people's state of mind, yet the state of their spiritual life must summon our most energetic love. It is just not good enough to wish our brothers' and sisters' souls well. By itself this is a lazy sort of kindness for those who follow the great Redeemer of Souls – who did and suffered so much in that great transaction. Not only must we *wish* them well, we have to work hard to *make* them well. That is why it is right to remind ourselves in all our dealings with other people of the supreme purpose of doing some good to their souls.

If this purpose were fixed in our minds we should find many opportunities which now we overlook of actually doing something. We might take the chance to teach God's way to someone who obviously doesn't know it well, to warn and advise someone who is openly sinning, to encourage and build up someone whose Christian living is faint and weak. Every spiritual need of a brother and sister can give us an opportunity to love him or her in this way.

Perhaps, in the circumstances, you think that it would not do any good to try yourself to help. You might think it presumptuous. You may not be sufficiently acquainted. These or other difficulties may render an approach ineffectual. Yet if yours is love in more than name only, you will most probably try to find someone else who can make a successful approach.

Bringing blessings to people's souls is such an important matter that, when direct ways are ruled out, we should use our wits to discover indirect ways. Surely it can't be right that we work harder at our own little worldly interests than at this great work of bringing spiritual blessings to other people? Yet we go at our own pursuits tirelessly, and we try one way after another to succeed.

Suppose that, after all your hard work, people are so obstinate they won't listen to you? Suppose you can't persuade them to have mercy on their own souls? You can still go on speaking to them by your example. Let your concern for them and the kindness of your own soul impress on them the value of theirs, and don't give up loving them. Weep in secret for them (Jeremiah 13.17, Psalm 119.136). Weep, as Jesus did (Luke 19.42), for those who do not know what will bring them peace. And when pleading with them won't work, still don't give up pleading with God for them. When Samuel could not dissuade the people from the evil course they had set their hearts on, he still insisted that he would not stop praying for them. In fact he took it on as a duty. He said that it would be sinful for him to stop praying.

> The Lord forbid that I should sin against him by no longer praying for you. (1 Samuel 13.23)

We need never feel that our prayers are wasted, for even if they are not answered directly, they will eventually bring us blessing, because love has its own rewards.

Then we must consider the love which we should have towards our neighbours at the completely physical level. Jesus would never have said that we should be like the 'Good Samaritan' of Luke, chapter 10, if the Samaritan in the story had only been *sorry* for the wounded man. Of course, he *helped him* as well. Neither good wishes nor good words are much use in such situations.

> Suppose there are brothers or sisters who need clothes and don't have enough to eat. What good is there in your saying to them, 'God bless you! Keep warm and eat well!' – if you don't give them the necessities of life? So it is with faith: if it is alone and includes no actions, then it is dead. (James 2.15-17)

True enough, that sort of charity won't help their bodies. And it won't help your soul either! God is never going to think of it as charity. This matter of helping others in their physical need is so central to our faith that we find it at the top of the list of items by which we will be judged on the last day:

> Then the King will say to the people on his right, 'Come, you that are blessed by my Father! Come and possess the kingdom which has been prepared for you ever since the creation of the world. I was hungry and you fed me, thirsty and you gave me a drink; I was a stranger and you received me in your homes, naked and you clothed me; I was sick and you took care of me, in prison and you visited me.' (Matthew 25.34-36)

And there are fierce things said to those who do not show active love:

> Away from me, you that are under God's curse! Away to the eternal fire which has been prepared for the devil and his angels! I was hungry but you would not feed me, thirsty but you would not give me a drink; I was a stranger but you would not welcome me into your homes, naked but you would not clothe me; I was sick and in prison but you would not take care of me. (Matthew 25.41-43)

This chapter (Matthew 25) tells us what loving acts are required of us. There are frequent, and sometimes exceptional, opportunities to show our love for people – as with the Good Samaritan who found a wounded person and did not pass him by (Luke 10.33,34). We have a special responsibility to help those who are in danger of their life:

> Rescue those being led away to death; hold back those who are staggering towards slaughter. (Proverbs 24.11)

And it will be no excuse to say we didn't know anything about it, for God knows our most secret thoughts:

> You may say that it is none of your business, but God knows and judges your motives. He keeps watch on you; he knows. And he will reward you according to what you do. (Proverbs 24.12)

LOVE AND CHARITY

Our love for others must be shown by our attitude towards their property and prosperity. We are to help our neighbours, in any honest way, to improve their property and to look after it. There are many occasions for us to show this sort of love. Sometimes we can talk someone out of doing harm to our neighbours. Sometimes we can assist with advice and information. We might be able to help our neighbours to advantage themselves, or to avoid some potentially ruinous course of action. There are many opportunities for us to do our neighbours a good turn without any loss to ourselves. Even our rich neighbours – those who are as wealthy or more wealthy than ourselves – we should help in this way.

But other people who are less well off than ourselves have much more claim on our love. We must go beyond supplying their needs. We must give to them freely, and let them have things which belong to us:

> If anyone has material possessions and sees his brother in need but has no pity on him, how can the love of God be in him? (1 John 3.17)

As a man, your brother bears the image of God. So you can't pretend you have any love for God or man if you love your money so much that you are content to see your poor brother suffer, rather than part with anything you own to help him out.

> Do not forget to do good and to help one another because these are the sacrifices that please God. (Hebrews 13.16)

> Your gifts are like sweet-smelling offerings to God, a sacrifice which is acceptable and pleasing to him. (Philippians 4.18)

When you are charitable, God is very pleased. Charity has always been high in the church's estimation; so much so that it has been linked with the most profound part of our worship – the Lord's Supper, where the collection is dedicated to the poor. Such charity is called in the Bible 'a sacrifice', as we see from these texts. But you will remember that sacrifices under the Old Testament law were often unacceptable because there was something wrong with them. Let's see, then, what could be wrong with our sacrifice of charity.

It might be the motive. Our first motive should be obedience and thankfulness to God. We can't pay God back in person for all he has done for us, so the poor 'stand in' for him as it were. The second motive must be true compassion, friendship and love for our neighbour; our desire for his comfort and relief. The third motive is the hope of the reward promised to us. Jesus reminds us of this when he tells us to,

> store up riches for yourselves in heaven. (Matthew 6.20)

and to

> make friends for yourselves with worldly wealth, so that when it gives out, you will be welcomed in the eternal home. (Luke 16.9)

What he means is that by giving generously from what we have in this world, we can store up for ourselves the blessings of heaven – the happiness which God has promised to those that show love to others. We can expect enough to compensate us entirely for what we give away, even if, as St Paul suggests, we

> give away everything we have. (1 Corinthians 13.3)

But we must not look for any other reward – not, for instance, for praise from other people. If we do that it will rob us of our heavenly reward.

> When you give something to a needy person, do not make a big show of it, as the hypocrites do in the houses of worship and on the streets. They do it so that people will praise them. I assure you, they have already been paid in full. But when you help a needy person, do it in such a way that even your closest friend will not know about it. Then it will be a private matter. And your Father, who sees what you do in private, will reward you. (Matthew 6.2-4)

And when we give, we must give cheerfully. When we give happily and with a good grace, those to whom we give value it much more than if we were to give grudgingly. God feels the same way:

God loves the one who gives gladly. (2 Corinthians 9.7)

Generosity is not a heartless rule from God; there's no more pleasurable duty. Doesn't it give us the greatest pleasure to see people who are poor getting joy out of being given some money? It lifts them up and gives them new life and hope just as they were sinking. Even the most pleasure-seeking people don't know where they can buy such satisfaction as this. So it really shouldn't be very hard for us to give – not grudgingly, but quickly and cheerfully.

But supposing we had to make ourselves poor in order to make others rich? Surely there is no pleasure in that? Just the thought might well stop us from giving anything at all. Yet if God commands it, we have to obey cheerfully in this matter as in any other. And didn't Jesus say,

None of you can be my disciple unless he gives up everything he has? (Luke 14.43)

Besides, there is no need to fear losing out, because God has promised blessings to those who give generously.

Be generous, and you will be prosperous. Help others, and you will be helped. (Proverbs 11.25)

Give to the poor and you will never be in need. If you close your eyes to the poor, many people will curse you. (Proverbs 28.27)

There are many more texts like this which show that our reservations about giving arise from our lack of faith. Put simply, we dare not trust God.

Think of giving to the poor as putting your wealth in God's hands:

When you give to the poor, it is like lending to the Lord, and the Lord will pay you back. (Proverbs 19.17)

If you refused to trust someone with money, he would take it as a personal insult. It would imply you thought that he was inadequate and couldn't pay you back – or that he was plain dishonest. What an affront it is not to trust God then! Worse, it's blasphemy, because God is Lord of all and all-sufficient; he is the God of truth and will not break his promise.

So then, don't let the fear that you might be in need in the future if you give away now, stop you from being kind to your poor brother. Though he may never pay you, yet God becomes his guarantor and will most certainly pay you back – with interest. So, far from sustaining a loss, you will be in profit. Any sensible person would rather put his money in reliable hands than leave it to be eaten away by inflation – or stolen! As it is, everything we possess could be lost to us at any moment, yet we could put it out of reach of inflation or accident by lending it to God. Then we shall be sure that it will be there when we need it, with interest added.

St Paul (2 Corinthians 9.10) compares our giving to sowing seed. When we give to those in need it's like sowing; what we give comes back to us – not just as we gave it, but more, a full harvest. God pays back richly, so we have every reason to be happy when we do our duty by the poor and help our neighbours in their need.

Next, we must take our opportunities. In the case of some who are in extreme poverty, every moment is the right one. They need help all the time because they are always in need. Yet, even then, there may be a special opportunity for helping them to the greatest advantage. Sometimes you can do more than just help people out of a present emergency; by carefully choosing the right time to give, you can help them towards making a living for themselves afterwards.

But, for the most part, the sooner we give the better. As soon as we decide to help we should do it. You wouldn't think much of a doctor who diagnosed an illness and decided on the best cure, but delayed helping you and kept you in pain! Yet that's just what we do if, by failing to help, we let a poor person in need have one hour of unnecessary suffering. There is another reason why we shouldn't delay: Satan can take the opportunity of tempting us away from our good intention. If you know you are inclined to be mean, be extra careful of putting off your charity.

We must give sensibly – where our help is most needed, and in a way that will do the recipient most good. You can go wrong if you don't take care. If you give away money automatically, you will inevitably give more to people who are lazy and beggarly than those who really need your help. You could encourage the lazy person to be idle; the help you give him could go to another with better effect. If things are really bad even the most unworthy person must be helped, but where there is no pressing need it is better to be selective – helping those who are not able to work, or whose expenses are much higher than their income.

We must give carefully to help people at their point of need. In some cases it will be better to give little by little, in others all at once. Sometimes a loan at the right time will be just as good as a gift – that can be done by those who can't afford to give away very much. But when we do make charitable loans, it must be without condition or interest. We should decide beforehand that if the one we are lending to can't pay back, we will forgive him as much of the money as he still needs and our circumstances will allow. It seems wrong to take legal action against people who can't pay back a debt, because there is nothing we can gain from it.

We must give generously. We must not be mean in our charity, or give in such little amounts that we might as well not have bothered. That's not charity, it's mockery! It's like pretending to feed someone who is starving by giving him a bread crumb. It's sub-Christian. Even John the Baptist – only the herald of Christ – insisted,

> Whoever has two shirts must give one to the man who has none, and whoever has food must share it. (Luke 3.11)

John is applying this principle not just to those who have vast arrays of clothing, but right down to someone who has only two coats. Even he has to part with one of them. From this we gather that, if we have more than we need, we should give it away when we see someone who can do with it. If we read carefully the story of the early church, we'll find that the first Christians gave even more generously than John's suggested proportion (one out of two coats):

> The group of believers was one in mind and heart. No one said that any of his belongings was his own, but they all shared with one another everything they had. (Acts 4.32)

And though they were in special circumstances – we are not in a position to do exactly as they did – yet it does demonstrate how fundamental charity is as a part of Christian behaviour; at the very founding of the church it was practised to such a sacrificial degree.

Think, too, of the rules of love given in the gospel:

> Christ gave his life for us. We too, then, ought to give our lives for our brothers! (1 John 3.16)

If God wants us to sacrifice our *lives* for our brothers, he'll certainly want us to be generous with our *goods*.

You know the grace of our Lord Jesus Christ; rich as he was, he made himself poor for your sake, in order to make you rich by means of his poverty. (2 Corithians 8.9)

Christ emptied himself of all the glory and greatness he enjoyed in heaven, and he submitted to a life of hardness and poverty, with the one purpose of enriching us. Shame on us! Let's reduce our bank balance a bit, and give a few things away to help other members of his body.

Remember that the person who sows few seeds will have a small crop; the one who sows many seeds will have a large crop. (2 Corinthians 9.6)

We wouldn't think much of a farmer who was so mean that he sowed insufficient seed to bring him a proper crop. And we shall be just as foolish if, by being mean, we end up with a poor harvest in eternity.

I am making no attempt to say by what proportion we should give; there are degrees of generosity. One person can give generously, and yet another can give even more generously. Besides, generosity is measured not so much by what is given as by how little the giver has to give. Somebody who has little money can be far more generous than another who is rich:

Jesus looked round and saw rich men dropping their gifts into the Temple treasury, and he also saw a very poor widow dropping in two little copper coins. He said, 'I tell you that this poor widow put in more than all the others. For the others offered their gifts from what they had to share of their riches; but she, poor as she is gave all she had to live on.' (Luke 21. 1-4; Mark 12.41-44)

Everybody must decide for themselves by what proportion they should give. Although St Paul presses the Corinthians to give, he doesn't tell them how much they should give, but leaves it to their own consciences:

Each one should give, then, as he has decided. (2 Corinthians 9.7)

But let's still remember that the more we give, the more acceptable it will be to God; and more he will reward us. If we follow St Paul's advice, our giving will be certain and reliable:

Every Sunday each of you must put aside some money, in proportion to what he has earned. (1 Corinthians 16.2)

If people did this every week they would never be without something to give when the opportunity arose. By putting a little aside
at a time, the expense would be less noticeable, and they wouldn't
begrudge giving away larger sums when they had to.

This practice also suits wage-earners and businessmen very
well, because they have a weekly check on their income and can
work out what their profit has been. That's the best time for them
to decide on their gift to God, so it can be in proportion to the
amount God has blessed them. If you say you can't work it out on a
weekly basis, so be it. I'll not argue with you about the precise
period of time. Let it be done monthly or quarterly – as long as it's
done! It's still better to put money aside regularly – into an account
if you like – than to give casually from money you happen to have
around. I assure you that if you tried it you would find it worked
very well.

EXERCISING MERCY

If we know someone to be innocent and he is slandered – even
called to account for something he hasn't done – charity demands
that we do what we can for him. Not only must we agree to be a
witness to his innocence if we are asked, but we should voluntarily
offer our testimony on his behalf. If our neighbour isn't being tried
by a court, but by malicious or casual gossip tossed from one
person to another, then we must do what we can to clear his name.
We should take all public opportunity to declare him innocent.

Even if our neighbour is guilty when he is accused, there is still a
charitable duty. If he really has done wrong and we are not obliged
to disclose it out of care for other people, then we should keep quiet.
Wounds to a person's reputation are the hardest of all to heal. So it
may well become our Christian duty to prevent them even where
they have been deserved. If we are kind to people in this way, and
hide their faults, it will quite possibly bring them to be sorry for
what they have done – especially if we give them private warning
and advice about it.

Let us suppose that the fault can't be concealed. There's still a
place for charity in lessening the consequences, as far as the
situation allows.

The most likely cirucumstances in which you might be able to
express this neighbourly love is when a friend or neighbour comes
under suspicion and yet you don't really know whether he is guilty
or innocent. Then you must remember that love thinks no evil – it

thinks the best of people. Don't jump to any uncharitable conclusions. Remember, reputations can be damaged quite as much
by unjustified suspicions as by the truest accusation. Jesus says

> Do not judge others, so that God will not judge you. (Matthew 7.1)

Quite evidently God takes this whole matter much more seriously
than the world seems to. If we judge other people without mercy,
we can expect God's strict and severe censure upon us.

Now it's customary to look upon expressing love as somewhat
less important than obeying laws. People think of charities as being
purely voluntary, and congratulate themselves when they are
charitable. In the same way they never blame themselves when
they neglect to be charitable. But we forget that we love one
another by Christ's command, and therefore there is a sense in
which charity has become part of law. Love is commanded by God
just as much as proper behaviour.

> The only obligation you have is to love one another. Whoever
> does this has obeyed the Law. The commandments, 'Do not
> commit adultery; do not desire what belongs to someone else' –
> all these, and any others beside, are summed up in the one
> command, 'Love your neighbour as you love yourself.' If you
> love someone, you will never do him wrong; to love, then, is to
> obey the whole Law. (Romans 13.8-10)

We must check all our actions against this standard – loving our
neighbour as ourselves. Whenever our neighbour is in need, we
should think what we would do for ourselves if we were in a similar
situation. Then we should make sure that we do as much for our
neighbour – out of love for him. This is what St James calls the
'royal law';

> You will be doing the right thing if you obey the royal law which
> is found in the scripture, 'Love your neighbour as you love
> yourself.' (James 2.8)

Anyone who reckons himself to be Christ's subject must be ruled
by this law, doing everything to help another person that he would
do to help himself. There's nobody who doesn't want to have his
reputation defended, his pain relieved, or his poverty taken away.

MAKING PEACE

There is one more expression of love which we haven't covered, and yet it can have a bearing on all the others. I'm talking about being a peace-maker. A peace-maker is a blessing to himself – health and possessions – and to everyone around him, because strife and quarrelling ruins everything. Bringing people together to make peace is a most rewarding activity. We have Christ's word for it:

> Happy are those who work for peace; God will call them his children! (Matthew 5.9)

So take every opportunity to be a peace-maker. Use all your skill, try your hardest to make up grudges and quarrels between other people.

Don't let's just stop at restoring peace where there has been confrontation, but let's do our best to conserve peace where it could be threatened. Peace is a precious jewel – try to plant it in other people's minds as you talk with them. Watch for the possible occasions of breakdown of peace. Try to prevent the thoughtlessness and the little aggravations which make people fall out with each other. You can do this amongst friends and neighbours. It's much more easy to stop arguments early on than it is later, when the situation is really bad. A quarrel is like a fire; when it's only smouldering you might be able to smother it, but as it grows, the position becomes hopeless. Peace-keeping is important not only because it prevents conflict, but also because it stops all the sins which are most likely to be committed once conflict has broken out.

If you want to be a peace-maker you have to be a peaceable person yourself; for how can you to persuade others to do what you won't do? You will never convince them. They will quickly say to you,

> Hypocrite! First take the log out of your own eye. (Matthew 7.5)

So be sure you are qualified.

There's one aspect of peaceable behaviour that people undervalue. It's to do with going to law. People take legal action over every little thing and, as long as they are legally in the right, they never think there is anything wrong in it. But the true peace-maker is unwilling to do this – to upset a neighbour over trivialities. It's not the use of the law which is unchristian, but actions in defence of petty rights (which it wouldn't do us any harm to lose) that arise from minor arguments and bitter feelings. Worst of all is when people go to court for revenge. Even when a dispute is of great importance, if you part with some of your rights because you love peace, you behave as a true Christian. St Paul says so:

> The very fact that you have legal disputes among yourselves shows that you have failed completely. Would it not be better for you to be wronged? Would it not be better for your to be robbed? (1 Corinthians 6.7)

However, if the damage is so unbearable that it's absolutely necessary for you to go to court, even then you must take care to keep the peace. It is still necessary to show a friendly and Christian attitude towards your oppponent. And, if there is some hope of agreement on reasonable terms, you should yield as soon as these terms are offered.

Take note of what I say, any of you who take pleasure in upsetting your neighbours or inducing others to do it, for the love of peace in ourselves and amongst others is the mark of servants of the 'Prince of Peace' (Isaiah 9.6), which we truly are.

What are the dimensions of love? To whom should we be charitable? Love takes in not only those we know, but strangers too – and even our most bitter enemies. I have already said how important it is for Christians to forgive, but let me take it one step further and suggest that we positively do good turns to our enemies. For, once we have forgiven them, we can no longer consider them enemies, so, humanly speaking, it will be much easier to be kind to them. Moreover, this is how we test the sincerity of our forgiveness. It is easy to say, 'I forgive so-and-so.' But if you refuse the first chance of doing him some good, that old hatred is still lurking in your heart. If you have entirely forgiven an enemy, you'll be as completely ready to help him as you would any friend. Indeed you might find it a greater joy and especially rewarding to be given the opportunity to show how sincere your reconciliation is, and at the same time obey your Saviour who said,

> Love your enemies, do good to those who hate you. (Luke 6.27)

There is another and higher reason. Christ did not only give us orders, nor did he simply have a change of heart towards us his most obdurate and provocative enemies. He showed his love in what he *did*. And what he did was neither cheap nor easy, but cost him his life-blood. We shall never successfully pretend to obey his command or follow his example if we grudgingly refuse to love our enemies in practice. Especially since what we have to do for them (outlined for us by St Paul in Romans 12.20) is so much less than anything he did for us.

If only we could bring ourselves to show practical kindness to our enemies, we might take away all their aggressiveness and bring them peace. The love we showed to them would then be doubled. This is what we should aim at. Those 'hot coals' which St Paul speaks about would not be coals to burn, but to melt our enemies into love and understanding towards us. That would truly be the best way of taking Christ's example. For in all he did and suffered for us, he worked to reconcile us to himself.

Vital to our service of love to our neighbours is the removal from our hearts of any selfishness. Love for ourselves often possesses us so completely that there is no room for charity for our neighbour – nor justice either. By this self-love I don't mean the quite proper love of ourselves which is the love and care of our souls, I mean the uncontrolled selfish love of our own worldly interests and advantages. Selfishness seems to be the root of all unjust and unloving behaviour towards other people. St Paul puts selfishness high on the list of sins:

> In the last days, people will be lovers of themselves, lovers of money, boastful, proud, abusive, disobedient to their parents, ungrateful, unholy, unkind, unforgiving, slanderous, without self-control, brutal, unjust, treacherous, reckless, swollen with pride, seeking pleasure rather than God, holding to an outward form of our religion but rejecting its real power. (2 Timothy 3.1-5)

See selfishness there at the head of the list as if it were some chief officer in Satan's army. And there's good reason for that, for it never goes about without a battalion of other sins, causing havoc and obliterating all thought of duty to others. Selfishness makes us so determined on our own pleasure that we take little notice of anybody else. We forget that St Paul tells us to behave in quite the opposite way:

> We should not please ourselves; instead, we should all please our brothers for their own good, in order to build them up in the faith, for Christ did not please himself. (Romans 15.1-3)

If we want genuine love for others, we must weed out selfishness; for they can't both grow together.

Even so, when we are rid of selfishness, we must remember that the ability to love doesn't come from ourselves. It is, like every other grace, a gift from God. Pray for it; pray that God will send his

Holy Spirit who once appeared in the form of a dove – a humble and guileless creature – that he might work in our hearts and bring us God's love so that we can serve him truly.

4

Conclusion

Jesus said, 'What do the scriptures say? How do you interpret them?' The man answered, 'Love the Lord your God with all your heart, with all your soul, with all your strength, and with all your mind; Love your neighbour as you love yourself.' Jesus replied, 'You are right, do this and you will live.' (Luke 10.26-28)

I have now shown you our duty to God, ourselves, and our neighbour. Surely, it is not impossible for us to do our duty in such a way that God will accept it; that is sincerely – though not of course perfectly. God is not like a cruel and over-demanding master. He is not like the 'hard man who takes what is not his and reaps what he did not sow' (Luke 19.21). Anything he asks us to do he will be willing to help us with. We shall please him as long as we're not lacking in prayerfulness or carefulness.

Our duty to God is not impossible. Nor is it such a boring task as people try to make out. Satan does what Joshua's spies did: 'spread a false report' (Numbers 13.32). They wanted to keep the people out of the promised land, and Satan too wants to discourage us from entering into God's promised land. Don't let's be cheated so easily! Let's at least have the courage to try, and we shall find it a land flowing with milk and honey. God's service doesn't take away pleasures, it opens up many of them. The work he wants to give us is acceptable, joyful and rewarding. What difficulty there is comes in subduing our own sinful attitudes and habits; when we get a grip on ourselves we realise it has been worth the trouble.

But someone objects that true devotion to God exposes us to persecution and suffering in the world! – these can't be pleasurable. Let me answer that even here there is joy to be had. Certainly the apostles experienced such joy:

They were happy, because God had considered them worthy to suffer disgrace for the sake of Jesus. (Acts 5.41)

And Peter said,

> If you suffer because you are a Christian, don't be ashamed of it
> but thank God that you bear Christ's name. (1 Peter 4.16)

The power and the goodness of a clear conscience, and the confidence it brings, can transform the greatest suffering into the
highest triumph. And that truth is never more clear and alive than
when we suffer in a true cause. So, you see, the Christian faith is
kind to us even in its saddest moments. And its inner joys far
exceed its outward pains. Despite the wars in which we find
ourselves on earth, the heavenly victory is sure, and our hope and
reward are eternal.

So, whenever we have a setback, we'll remember this rich prize
and...

> run with determination the race that lies before us. Let us keep
> our eyes fixed on Jesus, on whom our faith depends from
> beginning to end. He did not give up because of the cross! On the
> contrary, because of the joy that was waiting for him, he thought
> nothing of the disgrace of dying on the cross, and he is now
> seated at the right-hand side of God's throne. Think of what he
> went through; how he put up with so much hatred from sinners!
> So do not let yourselves become discouraged and give up.
> (Hebrews 12.1,2,3)

Christ's promise of the crown of life can keep a Christian in prison
more happy than a man of the world in the middle of all his riches.

I have nothing further to add but this: 'Please, please, start
walking along this way of Christian duty without hesitation.' Put
into practice what you have read in this book or learned by any
other means. The further off-course you are, the more quickly you
need to get back on the road; and the more care you need to take as
you travel along.

Imagine you are on a journey and you have a long way to go.
Suddenly you find you have lost time by going the wrong way! You
won't need much encouragement either to get back on the right
way or to speed up. This is the situation of all who have set out on a
sinful course. They are on the wrong road, and it will never take
them where they need to go. Worse, it will most certainly bring
them to the place they most fear.

The day is far spent, and no one knows how much time is left to
finish the journey. Dying comes – when? – tonight? The next hour?
the next minute? Why wait a second longer to get off the sinner's
road? It most certainly leads to eternal death. Get on the road to

happiness and glory!

Yet people are so bewitched, enthralled and deceived by sin, that no-one can beg them – nothing can persuade them – to change. Such a logical and necessary change! – they even agree that it is. Yet, they are unwilling to do anything about it. They want to leave everything to the last moment and jump on to heaven's hill. But it's a long way up and the climb is gradual. It takes time.

You have read all the arguments that might persuade you to act, but I will leave you with this one thought,

> Don't think that you can keep putting it off. Come back to the Lord right now! (Ecclesiasticus 5.7)

5

A Selection of Prayers from 'The Whole Duty of Man'

PRAYERS IN THE MORNING

LORD, WAKE ME FROM MY SIN

Lord,
Wake me up from my sin,
just as you woke me this morning to a new day.
Today let me walk with you;
and walk with you through all the rest of my life.
Then, when that trumpet of eternity sounds
wake me up for ever, to life without end,
to be with you always.

Amen.

HELP ME . . .

Lord,
I don't know what to pray for as I should.
Let your Spirit help me in my weakness
to offer myself a spiritual sacrifice
acceptable to you through Jesus Christ.

Amen.

THANK YOU...

. . . *For loving me*

Lord of love,
your kindness never ends.
I am full of your love for me,
and so I want to offer you my humblest praise.
I live and move and exist because of you, O Lord.

. . . *For making me yours*

First you made me;
and then you made me happy
by sending your Son – you loved him so much! –
to prise me from the grip of my sins.
His blood saved me
    from the punishment I deserved.
His innate goodness and his sacrifice – his death –
will bring me to glorious life for ever.
It was you who brought me to birth
    in the faith of Christ.
I was consecrated to you in baptism,
brought within the family of your Church.
I have shared in Christian knowledge and worship,
drawing strength from them
so that I might keep the promises made to you.

...For forgiving me

Time and again I let you down –
sometimes deliberately, sometimes without thinking –
yet you love me, and you never fail me.
Every time, you open the way for me to say sorry.
Every time, you give me the chance
   to show how sorry I am.
You have endless patience with me, Lord!
You could have judged me straight away
for the things I had been doing;
that's what I deserved.
In fact it is only because you held me back
that I did nothing worse!
And it is only because you guide and help me
that I can do any good at all.
So you must have the praise, not me.
for every spiritual blessing,

...For caring for me

   'My soul praises the Lord!'
   (Luke 1.46; Psalm 103.1)

Let me praise you, Lord,
for the physical blessings I enjoy;
health, friends, food, and clothes –
the comforts as well as the necessities of life.
Let me praise you, Lord,
for keeping me and mine from danger.
In every emergency
you have helped me out.
Such troubles as you have let happen to us
you have lifted and eased,
even if you have not taken them away altogether.
Let me praise you, Lord,
for caring for me during this past night,
and for every other goodness towards me.

Amen.

LORD, LET ME PRAISE YOU

Lord, let me praise you
not only by the words I say,
but by the way I live.
Help me do what you tell me,
so that my life may be
just a taste of the delights
you have ready for those who love you,
through Jesus Christ our Lord.

Amen.

I AM SO VERY SORRY

I have been rebellious

Righteous Lord, you hate sin:
I want to throw myself at your feet.
I know what I really deserve –
that you should be disgusted with me
and leave me altogether.
I have drunk sin like water.
My rebelling against you has gone on a long while.
I have done the things which you said I shouldn't do;
I have not done the things that you told me to do.
My heart should be a palace for your Spirit,
but it has become a dirty hovel
full of sordid and perverse loves.
And the trouble is
that I find my mouth saying
and my hands doing
the very things that I'm thinking about.
Thinking, speaking, and doing,
I keep sinning against you.

(Here tell God the worst of your sins)

I have been hard

O Lord,
you have been so good to me,
giving me the chance and the way
    to put things right.
But I have been hard;
I haven't listened to you.
And so, Lord, what can I expect you to do?
except to judge me and be fiercely angry with me.
That is what I truly deserve.

Make me a new person

But, O Lord,
I know that you can be merciful.
O make me fit for your mercy! –
give me a deep and heartfelt repentance.
Then be good to me again;
take your anger and your fury away from me.
Look at me in your Son, my wonderful Saviour.
And because he deserves it, not me,
through his sufferings forgive all my sins.
And, Lord,
I pray that your love will give to me
a new and clean life.
Make me a new person!
Help me to give up every evil way.
Every day help me to obey you –
constantly, sincerely, in everything,
and all the rest of my life.
So may I,
as a good and faithful servant,
in the end share the joy of my Lord.
Answer my prayer for Jesus Christ's sake.

Amen.

LET YOUR LIGHT SHINE IN

Make me long to do your will

O God, you give so wonderfully
to me so undeserving.
Without you I can't even think a good thought.
Come to me and make me long to do your will.
Open the windows of my mind that I may see and
    know you.
Let your light shine in and bring that knowledge
    to fruition.
Lord, grow a true faith in my heart,
a hope that keeps me clean and good,
an unpretended love to you.
Make me trust you completely.

I am your servant

Give me enthusiasm for serving you,
and a deep respect for everything that belongs to you.
Make me careful not to hurt you.
Make me thankful for your love to me.
Help me to take it humbly when you correct me.
Make me keen to worship you, and sorry for my sins.
Lord, help me to remember I am your creature.
Help me to serve you well. I am your servant.
And, Lord, I have a duty to my character:
give me serenity, humility,
contentedness, patience
and thankfulness.
In all I do make me careful.
Keep my eyes open to temptation.
Keep me holy, keep me gentle.
Stop me being extravagant in my pleasures –
don't let them ever become a trap for me.

Help me to love
And Lord,
I don't want to break this royal law of yours:
to love my neighbour as myself;
help me so to love.
Lord, I want to be as kind to everyone as you were.
Whether with friends or enemies, you command love.
So give me real love and sympathy deep down inside.
And the last thing, Lord:
make me holy every bit,
all through and all the way;
so that when the Lord Jesus comes,
I may not offend him –
not in mind or body or spirit.
Father, to you and to our Lord Jesus
    and to your Holy Spirit
be all honour and glory, always.

Amen.

FOR EVERYONE WHO NEEDS GOD

Our race

Heavenly Lord,
you care for everything you have made:
have mercy on all the human race.
Your Son, on the cross, paid the ransom-price for all.
Let this love save all – in reality.
People are in darkness –
light up their dark sky.
People are set in their sinful ways –
turn them round by your grace.

Our church

Love your church with tenderness, O Lord.

'O God be kind to Zion and help her;
rebuild the walls of Jerusalem'
(Psalm 51.18)

Bring together all who say they are Christians:
bring them to yourself
in goodness and godliness;
bring them to each other
with the love of brothers and sisters.

Our nation

Have mercy on our empty churches.
Have mercy on our sinful nation.
You have shaken our land and divided it; heal our wounds.
We tremble before you.
Where we deserve your judgement,
make us sorry for our sins.
Forgive us and bless us.

Our leaders

Bless the leaders of our church
and the leaders of our nation.
Let them govern with a true heart and a strong hand.
Give them the will and the power
to remove evil and crime,
and to bring in faith and goodness.

Our neighbours

Lord, be generous to those in distress:
be father to the fatherless,
be companion to the grieving:
strengthen the confused in mind,
hold up the weak,
heal those who are ill,
bring relief to the poor,
defend the victimised.
O Lord of love, meet everyone's need.

Our family

For those who are near or dear to us,
we ask for your blessing:

(Here, name your nearest relations)

you know what is best for them in body and soul.

Give satisfaction to those who do good to us.
Forgive all those who have wished us harm.
Make them, and us, right in your eyes,
through Jesus Christ our Lord.

Amen.

IT'S A NEW DAY

Kind God,
there wouldn't be another day in my life
    it it were not for you.
Through all its hours, guide me by your love;
that I may do nothing which would dishonour you,
or wound my own soul.
Make me work carefully at all the good things
    that you have planned for me.
And Lord, I pray,
put your angels in charge of me
to look after me wherever I go.
Let nothing evil happen to me,
nor any curse come near where I live.
So shall I and mine be safe under your loving care,
through Jesus Christ.

Amen.

I NEED YOU

O Lord,
forgive my rambling prayers,
and my coldness towards you.
Please answer my prayers
not because I deserve it – I don't,
but because I need you
and because you love me in Jesus Christ.

Amen.

PRAYERS IN THE EVENING

I DON'T KNOW WHAT TO PRAY FOR . . .

Lord,
I don't know what to pray for as I should.
Let your Spirit help me in my weakness
to offer myself a spiritual sacrifice
acceptable to you through Jesus Christ.

Amen.

THINGS HAVE GONE BADLY

I have failed

O Lord God,
you will not look at sin because you are too holy.
How should I come before you? –
my soul is so polluted.
I am very slow to do good, very ready to do wrong.
It's my nature that is wrong.
But I have made things even worse
by deliberately sinning
and getting into wrong habits.
I have fallen short in my duty
to you, to my neighbour, and to myself.
I have failed in my thinking.
I have failed in what I have said and done.
You have told me not to do things,
    and I have done them,
you have asked me to do things,
    and I have not bothered.

I am so rebellious

It's not that I'm stupid or weak;
I know exactly what I am doing.
And I push against your Holy Spirit
and even against my own conscience,
to do exactly the oposite.
And this is worse:
I keep going wrong by the day and by the week,
despite your pleading with me,
and despite all my promises to do better.
My old sins were bad enough,
but even today I have added new ones:

(Here be specific)

So, Lord, what can I say?
I have done all these things wrong –
how can I speak to you?
I know that death is the wages sin pays,
but you do not want a sinner to die –
have mercy on me!
Lord, I want to be really sorry
and come to hate my sins.
I want to get out of this round of confessing my sins
and the next day doing them all again.

Please change me, Lord

O Lord, this very moment
divorce me from every wrong I cling to,
then wed me to yourself.
Make me true, good, and holy.
Let Jesus, who died on the cross for me,
bring me to you;
in him forgive all my sins,
for his sake put me right with you.
And when your words of peace have penetrated my soul,
Lord keep me,
that I may be no longer stupid.

Amen.

THANK YOU FOR YOUR LOVE –
I DON'T DESERVE IT

Kind Father,
caring for me must be a thankless task;
I know I have been very trying.
Every day I provoke you,
but you still shower your kindness on me.
Even though I have spurned you and ignored your gifts,
you have not stopped giving.
You just put up with me!
You go on offering me your love and life in Jesus.
Even though I have misused the things you have given me,
you have not punished me by taking them away.
You give me generously all I need.
You have not repaid today's sins
by wiping me off the face of the earth –
that would be the right punishment
    for one who has rejected you –
but you have spared me and kept me safe.
How great is your love!

(Here mention God's special gifts to you this day)

'What can I offer the Lord
    for all his goodness to me?'
    (Psalm 116.12)

Lord, let this goodness of yours lead me to repentance.
Let me not only thank you and praise you,
but behave myself properly too.
So may I at last see God's salvation
through Jesus Christ.

Amen.

PLEASE KEEP ME SAFE

Lord, you are
  'the protector of Israel
  who never dozes or sleeps'
  (Psalm 121.4)

Please protect me this night in your love.
Keep me from all evil things
and defend me from all danger.
Give me gentle, satisfying, and refreshing sleep,
to make me fit for what I have to do tomorrow.
And Lord, remind me that one day
I shall lie down to sleep for the last time.
And because I don't know
  when Jesus will come for me,
keep me always ready for him.
Let me never live so that I am afraid to die.
Lord, while I live,
let me live in you,
when I die,
let me die in you;
so that living or dying I may be yours,
through Jesus Christ.

Amen.

THE LAST PRAYER

O wonderful saviour,
when you died and when you were buried,
you took away the sting of death
and the power of the grave.
Let the results of your victory be mine:
be my victory in life and in death.

> 'When I lie down I go to sleep in peace;
> and alone, O Lord,
> keep me perfectly safe'
> (Psalm 4.8)

I offer my soul to your safe-keeping'
for you have bought it back,
Lord God of truth.

Amen.

PRAYERS FOR SPECIAL HELP

I PRAY FOR HOPE

Lord,
you are hope all the world over.
Build my hope on firm foundations;
keep me from being self-assured.
Let me never hope in myself.
Do not once permit me to think
that you will condone my sin.
Yet keep the hope strong
    that you will forgive me
when I come to you in sorrow
    for what I have done.
Lord, give me the kind of hope
that trusts your promises alone;
that makes me long to be holy.
So let me

> 'hold tight to the hope placed before us...
>   the anchor for our lives...
>   that is safe and sure
>   and goes through the curtain
>   of the heavenly temple
>   into the inner sanctuary
>   where Jesus is gone before us –
>   our high priest for ever.'
>   (Hebrews 6.18-20)

Amen.

LORD, HELP MY BELIEVING

Lord of all goodness, all praise, and all joy,

   'we cannot please you unless we trust you'.
   (Hebrews 11.6)

Let your Spirit move in me,
to engender a strong and loving faith;
so shall I make you glad.
Never leave me satisfied
   with a faith that is weak and useless.
Let what I believe be seen in what I do!
Give me a victorious faith;
a faith stronger than the attractions of the world,
a faith which can change me,
a faith which can make me like my Lord,
a faith which one day
   shall procure the salvation of my soul
in Jesus Christ,

Amen.

I WANT TO KNOW YOUR LOVE

Make me strong

Holy and loving Lord:
your greatness cannot be measured,
nor your love for me.
Keep the deceits of sin
from hardening my heart
   against the charms of your love.
Deep in my soul
set the imprint of your loving spirit.
Lord, you ask for my heart,
and only you have the right to it;
let me not so wrong you or offend you
as to reserve any part of it for myself.
But give me the strength to open all my heart to you.
Yet, Lord God,
you know that other things
have displaced you already;
you know that the world, with its flatteries,
has taken over
and holds on like a wrestler.

Possess me, Lord

O Lord, you are strong!
overcome my selfishness.
Take possession of my unworthy heart
as the spoil of your victory.
Refine my heart with your love's purifying fire;
make it fit for your Holy Spirit to live in.
Lord, if it is your will,
let me taste the joys which have thrilled your saints;
let me know the ravishing of your love.
And if I do not know what I am asking –
if I may not choose my own place in your kingdom,
yet, O Lord,
do not forbid me to drink the cup which you drink.

Give me a real love

Give me love so true and so full
that I may endure anything for your sake.
Give me love so complete
that it will cast out fear;
a love that makes nothing too hard to put up with,
a love that makes nothing too difficult to do,
a love which obeys your commands.
So may I at last
by your mercy wear the crown of life
which you have promised to those who love you,
through Jesus Christ our Lord.

Amen.

MAKE ME SINCERE

Holy Lord,
you want us to be people of truth and integrity:
save me from hypocrisy and from being insincere.
Hearts are deceitful,
and my heart is more deceitful than others.

> 'Lord, you search our minds
> and test our hearts'.
> (Jeremiah 17.10)

Try me, and find out what my heart is like.
Don't let any hateful thing hide there.
With your fire make me pure –
burn out this contamination.
    I can't deceive you, O, Lord;
keep me from deceiving myself!
Make me despise my hidden sins,
give me the strength to fight them.
Don't let me talk peace to myself,
when there is no peace.
So shall I deal with my life as you see me;
may I never be at peace with myself
until I am at perfect peace with you!
Then, pure in heart,
I shall see you in your kingdom.

Amen.

IMPROVE MY PRAYING

Give me strength

Kind Lord,
we are thankless creatures –
and we want so much!
Yet you permit us – more, you invite us –
to bring our requests to you.
Lord, give me the grace to pray
as often as I need you –
and how I need you!
Lord, I tell you it is a great honour,
and a great gift,
to be allowed to come close to you.
Yet so dull and stupid is my worldly heart,
that it will not take the opportunities I have.
Lord, my spirit is ill – crippled –
it just cannot lift itself up to you.

Give me concentration

Come, Lord, and cure this sad disease,
cure my infected heart.
Give it energy and life,
that I may rise to pray.
Let me take delight in coming to you.
Let me come to you with deference,
in deference to the majesty of your throne,
with an instancy,
an earnestness
matching my need;
with a mind so concentrated
that no stray thought may interrupt.

Give me determination

Let me not be guilty any more
of coming close to you with my lips
and keeping away from you with my heart;
or of going straight from my prayer to sin again.
Let me

> 'ask from you, that I may receive
> seek, that I may find;
> knock, that the door may be opened to me'.
> (Matthew 7.7,8)

Lord, teach me to pray to you here,
that in eternity I may praise you
   in your glory.
Answer me, Lord, for the sake of your Son;
because he is good – not me,
and because he pleads with you for me:
my Lord Jesus Christ.

Amen.

LORD, GIVE ME HUMILITY

'High and holy God
you live in eternity,
but you also live with people who are
humble and repentant'.
(Isaiah 57.15)

Drive out my pride

Pour into my heart humility – that supreme gift,
which can altogether displace
   the vain opinions I have of myself.

Show me how helpless I am

Lord,
forcibly convict me of my own poverty;
make me see that I am helpless,

   'poor, naked and blind'
   (Revelation 3.17) –

not only a child of dust, but also of sin.
So that if I become rich or poor in this life,
I can leave off being proud
and from my heart admit
that I deserve
less than the least of your gifts of love
and more than the greatest
   of your sentences of judgement.

Help me to accept criticism

And, Lord, help me to

   'live in humble fellowship with my God'
   (Micah 6.8)

and not only with my God,
but with other people too.
Give me the grace to submit
not only to your criticism,
but also to that of my fellow-Christians,
and humbly to heed their advice.
Lord, this is how I want to behave towards everybody:

'never to do anything from selfish ambition
or from a cheap desire to boast,
but to humble towards others,
always considering them better than myself'
(Philippians 2.3)

to let others look down on me if they will,
not to be opinionated
or to look for some particular praise
but, mistrusting the approval of men,
to seek only for your approval.

Help me to want to please only you

In the past, Lord,
I have used all ways to cultivate people's respect –
let it now be you I please,

'for you have no use
for conceited people,
but show favour to those who are humble'.
(Proverbs 3.34; James 4.6; 1 Peter 5.5)

O Lord, answer my prayer for humility
in the name of the one

'who was humble
and walked the path of obedience
all the way to death –
his death on the cross'
(Philippians 2.8)

Jesus Christ, my Lord.

Amen.

KEEP ME TRUSTING

Lord of all power,
you never fail those who trust in you.
Give me grace, I pray,
in every difficulty and danger
to turn to you,
to rest in you,
and to depend on you.

'You, Lord, give perfect peace
to those who keep their purpose firm
and put their trust in you'
(Isaiah 26.3)

Lord, help me found my life on this rock,
and never upon the frail structures of the world.
Keep my mind from being overburdened
with the anxieties of living:

'what I am to eat or drink,
or what clothes I should put on'
(Matthew 6.31)

Grant that when I have done everything I can –
working hard, working conscientiously –
I may happily give myself into your care

'not worrying about anything'
(Philippians 4.6)

'leaving all my cares with you'
(1 Peter 5.7)

Let this be my one concern:
to belong to you,
to be in the circle of your protection,
to be obedient to your laws;

'to remember your commandments and do them'
(Psalm 103.18)

Let me

'be concerned above everything else
with your kingdom,
and with what you require of me'
(Matthew 6.33)

that you may provide my other needs
as your wisdom knows best.
Grant this O Lord
for Jesus Christ's sake.

Amen.

GIVE ME REVERENCE

Lord of majesty,
you alone are supreme
you alone are to be worshipped.
Put my heart in awe of you,
that I may honour you as you deserve.
Make me have such high regard
for everything holy,
that I may never profane what is yours alone;
that I may never invade or intrude upon
what you have set apart for yourself.
And since you are a God

> 'who will not overlook the guilty'
>   (Exodus 34.7)

make the fear of your judgement
    keep me from provoking your anger.
Let my loyalties not be so misplaced
as to fear man,
    who will die like the grass
and yet forget the Lord my maker,
    who is eternal.
Fill my soul with

> 'the fear of the Lord'
> which is
> 'the beginning of wisdom'
>   (Psalm 111.10; Proverbs 9.10)

Hold back my basest desires
and free me to live for you.
Hear me O Lord, I beg you,
and put this awe in my heart,
so that I may never go far from you;
so that

> 'with fear and trembling...
> I may work out my own salvation'
>   (Philippians 2.12)

through Jesus Christ.

Amen.

MAKE ME GRATEFUL, LORD

O good and generous Lord:
to all of us you give,
and expect nothing in return
but praise and thanksgiving.
And that's the easiest thing we can give you!
Let me never deny it to you;
let my heart know your love,
and my mouth confess it.
Gratitude
is such a happy experience –
do not let me lose that God-given pleasure.
But as I receive your blessings every day,
so every day let me thank you
from an affectionate and devoted heart.
Let the praises I sing fill my life!
Let me dedicate myself to your service;
walking with you,
doing what is right,
being true to you all the days of my life;
through Jesus Christ,
my Lord and wonderful saviour.

Amen.

MAKE ME SORRY

Melt this hard heart of mine . . .

Holy Lord,
you welcome those who are sorry for their sin.
To the obstinate
you are a fire of judgement.
How dare I approach you?
I have done so many wrong things
that might make your anger burn,
and I show so little sorrow for what I have done.
Lord,
melt this hard heart of mine
that I may regret the sins in my life.

I have been asleep so long . . .

My heart is as a rock.
Like Moses in the wilderness,
who

> 'struck the rock and water flowed out'
> (Numbers 20.11)

so, Lord, strike my heart!
that floods of tears may wash my conscience clean.
Lord, I have been asleep for so long in my sin –
wake me with your thunder!
I would rather tremble at your power,
than tremble for my sins.
You sent your dear Son
to heal the broken-hearted.
But, Lord, what use is that to me,
if my heart was never broken?
O break me, so that I may be healed!
Lord, sin has turned sour on me;
sin is poison!
Let me run from it as from a scorpion.
Let repentance change my life!
Let my life glorify your grace
in Jesus Christ my redeemer.

Amen.

KEEP ME HUMBLE

Lord Jesus:
like a sheep led to slaughter
you were led out to die.
Let such humility
take from me all thought of anger or revenge.
Give me gentleness of character;
give me a calm
that no provocation can disturb.
Teach me not to retaliate
when people hurt me –
unless it be with prayers and love!
So may I, who have so many faults to be forgiven,
never condemn others.
Let me

> 'clothe myself with compassion, kindness,
>   humility, gentleness and patience'
>   (Clossians 3.12)

that you may live with me –
for you are the Prince of Peace.
To you be glory
with the Father and the Holy Spirit for ever.

Amen.

MAKE ME VIRTUOUS

Holy and perfect Jesus,
you delight to live in pure and unspoilt lives
Send your spirit of purity
to take away my uncleanness.
Let me never pollute my body,
which is the temple of the Holy Spirit,
with any uncleanness.
And let me keep well this heart
from which comes the things that defile me;
that I harbour no impure thought.
Help me O Lord to keep my life pure and undefiled;
so that here I may glorify you,
and in body and spirit be glorified
    with you in eternity.

Amen.

PLEASE CONTROL MY APPETITE

Kind Lord, good to all,
you have given us freedom in your world,
using your creation to sustain our lives.
This freedom let me employ gratefully,
and with care.
Keep me from slavery to appetite,
where eating becomes a trap.
Make me moderate in consumption;
eating and drinking for health's sake –
and not for luxury.
Let me live
not for failing pleasures,
but for those things which last for ever.
Make me hungry and thirsty to do right.
So may I be filled with your grace here,
and with your glory in eternity,
through Jesus Christ.

Amen.

MAKE ME CONTENTED

O God,
in your wisdom you choose,
and in your love you provide
good things for us.
Make me contented –
not hankering after my own way,
but completely satisfied
with your choices for me.
Let me

> 'learn to be content whatever the circumstances'
> (Colossians 4.11)

not resenting my own state of life,
nor envying that of others.
Free my heart from covetousness;
help me to defend myself against the love of money.
Whether I become rich or poor,
make me so contemptuous of riches
that I never set my heart on them;
but only long to be rich towards God,

> 'storing up for myself treasures in heaven'
> (Matthew 6.20)

Let me

> 'set my heart upon the things that are in heaven'

so that

> 'my real life is Christ
> and, when he appears,
> then I will appear with him
> and share his glory'
> (Colossians 3.1,4)

Through him I bring my prayer to you, O Lord.

Amen.

GIVE ME ENTHUSIASM

Lord of wisdom
you have so ordered the world,
that we are born to a life of work.
Keep me from laziness –
from rejecting your plan for me.
Let me use my time and talents well,
so that I shall not be condemned
like the

> 'wicked, lazy servant'
> (Matthew 25.26)
> of the parable.

Lord, show me
how you would have me serve other people
and show me how
> 'to make God's call
> and his choice of me
> a permanent experience'
> (2 Peter 1.10)

Lord, my spiritual enemies are wide awake;
I am surrounded by great danger.
Don't let me go to sleep!
Make me

> 'watch and pray
> so that I do not fall to temptation'
> (Matthew 26.41)

Make me

> 'endure hardship like a good soldier
> of Jesus Christ'
> (2 Timothy 2.3)

until, by your power,
the battle of this world becomes at last
the triumph and glory of your kingdom;
through Jesus Christ.

Amen.

LET ME BEHAVE JUSTLY

Let me be conscientious

Just and holy Lord:
you have comanded us to do right,
and to see that right is done.
Free my heart and my hands
from all dishonesty and wrong-doing.
Give me integrity;
make me straight-forward in all my dealings.
Keep me in dread of using my power
    to oppress my brother,
and of using my skill to deceive him.
Make me more careful to keep this sacred rule:

> 'treat others
>   as you would have them treat you'
>   (Luke 6.31)

Let me be blameless

Let me never let you down
by living dishonestly.
But let me behave in this world
with simplicity and Godly sincerity;
not looking to amass wealth –
preferring only to have enough and be behave justly
rather than to be a millionaire and dishonest.
My debts, let me pay scrupulously;
my contracts, let me honour without default.
So let me behave in front of other people,
that no evil criticism can be levelled at me;
that I may live at peace with everyone.
So let me behave before God –
innocently, truthfully –
that I may have peace at the last with him
through Jesus Christ our Lord.

Amen.

GIVE ME LOVE IN MY HEART…

Make me loving

O Lord of love:
you have made us all alike,
and you have offered salvation to all
by one act of redemption.
Let me never harden my heart against those
　　who share with me the same nature
and to whom you have offered the same salvation.
But grant me an undiscriminating love
　　towards all men.

Make me compassionate

Compassionate Father,
bring me such warmth and tenderness of heart
that I may be deeply affected by sorrows
　　and disasters
which come to other people,
and put all my skills to work
to bring them help and relief.
Keep from my heart the spirit of self-love,
which is anti-Christ.
Drive out that cursed spirit!
and let your spirit of love for others
enter and live there.

Make me concerned

Make me concerned to please my neighbour;
to do good to him
rather than just to myself –
for Jesus did not love to please himself.
Lord make me

> 'a reliable and wise manager'
>   (Luke 12.42)

of such skills as you have given me
for the assistance of others;
so that, when you ask me
what I have done in your service,
I may tell you with joy, and not with tears.
Please answer my prayer, O loving Lord,
for the sake of Jesus Christ.

Amen.

LORD, I WANT TO BE STRONG

I am weak

Eternal and unchanging Lord God,
you are

'the same yesterday, today and for ever'
(Hebrews 13.8)

Grant something of your permanence, your stability
to my inconsistent life.
I am weak, and I waver;
my soul is light and blown about.
My mind is easily deceived –
O Lord, found it on your truth,
keep it from traps of evil persuasion;
that I may not be led away by the wicked
and fall from my strength.
Lord, I am irresolute and indecisive
because I do not cling tight to you.
My love for you

'disappears as quickly as the morning mist;
it is like the dew, that vanishes early in the day'
(Hosea 6.4)

Be my shield

O build me up and make me stong.
And whatever good you have been pleased
   to do through me,
go on doing it until Christ comes.
Lord, you see my weakness,
and you know the temptations I struggle with –
their power, and how many they are.
Please do not leave me
   to defend myself on my own,
but you be my shield in the heat of the battle.
And in every spiritual fight
let me

   'triumph through Christ who loves me!'
   (Roman 8.37)

Help me to stand firm

Let neither fear nor flatttery,
nor my own selfish desires,
ever induce me to disobey you.
But help me

   'to stand firm in faith unyielding,
     working steadily and well for the Lord'
   (Corinthians 15.58)

and through a lifetime of patience in doing good,
to come at last
to an eternity of glory and honour,
through Jesus Christ our Lord.

Amen.

THE LORD'S PRAYER

(Matthew 6.9-14, etc)

'OUR FATHER IN HEAVEN'

O Lord,
you live in the highest heaven;
you are the author of our being.
By you we are born again
with the hope of life.
You love us, you are kind to us – like a caring father.
Help us give back to you the love of obedient children,
so that we may be like you, our Father in Heaven.
Give us a dislike of what seem like pleasures,
but are really the polluted things of this world.
So raise up our thoughts
that we may always have heaven in our minds;
for from heaven we look for our saviour
and Lord Jesus Christ to come.

Amen.

'HALLOWED BE YOUR NAME'

Make us respectful to you
so let us honour your name.
Your name is great and wonderful and holy.
Give us reverence for everything that belongs to you,
especially for the worship of your Church;

> 'Let all the people praise you, O God!
> Let all the people praise you'
> (Psalm 67.3,5)

Amen.

'YOUR KINGDOM COME'

Set up your power and rule for ever in our lives.
Put down all those rebel wrongs in our nature
    that set themselves up against you –
they are your enemies
    and do not want you to rule over them.
Bring them to justice!
And make us such faithful subjects of your kingdom here
that one day we may become
subjects of your glorious kingdom.
So,

'Lord Jesus, come quickly!'
  (Revelation 22.20)

Amen.

'YOUR WILL BE DONE ON EARTH, AS IN HEAVEN'

Lord,
by your grace help us to accept happily
everything you plan for us
and to do
everything you want us to do.
Give us the enthusiasm of the angels in your presence
that we may be quick to respond to your will
and vigorous in doing it.
So that, obeying you all our days,
we may praise you in eternity.

Amen.

'GIVE US TODAY OUR DAILY BREAD'

Give us a continual supply of your goodness,
which will feed and strengthen our souls
for eternal life;
give us all things which we need
for our journey on earth.
Help us to rely on you,
and to accept cheerfully what you send,

> 'concerned above everything else
> with the Kingdom of God,
> and with what he requires of us,
> and not doubting that he will provide us
> with all these other things'
> (Matthew 6.33)

Amen.

'FORGIVE US OUR SINS, AS WE FORGIVE THOSE WHO SIN AGAINST US'

Heal us, Lord,
for we have sinned against you.
Love us tenderly
and forgive all our sin.
Lord, may we never lose forgiveness
by failing to forgive one another.
Give us that compassion for each other
which we so much need from you.
As Jesus commands,
let us forgive
just as fully and completely as we need to be forgiven.
For we are only forgiven
because of his prayers and his deserving.

Amen.

'LET US NOT BE LED INTO TEMPTATION

O Lord,
we are weak in the face of many temptations
that confront us everyday.
But our eyes are on you.
Please restrain these temptations
or help us through them.
You have promised
that our testing will not be more than we can bear.
From all our temptations give us a way out,
so they don't get the better of us.

In our

> 'struggle against sin, we
> have not yet resisted
> to the point of shedding our blood'
> (Hebrews 12.4)

But if you call us to fight
help us to be faithful to you,

> 'even if it means death',

so that you will give us

> 'life as your prize of victory'
> (Revelation 2.10)

Amen.

'FOR THE KINGDOM, THE POWER, AND THE GLORY ARE YOURS'

Hear our prayers and answer them,
for you are the great ruler of all the earth.
Your power is infinite,
and you are able to do for us
more than we are able to ask or think.
If any of the good that you work in us brings glory,
it belongs to you.
therefore,

> 'to him who sits on the throne to the Lamb
> to praise and honour and glory and power,
> for ever and ever!'
> (Revelation 5.13)

Amen.